USN FLEET DESTROYER
VS
IJN FLEET SUBMARINE

The Pacific 1941–42

MARK STILLE

OSPREY PUBLISHING
Bloomsbury Publishing Plc
PO Box 883, Oxford, OX1 9PL, UK
1385 Broadway, 5th Floor, New York, NY 10018, USA
E-mail: info@ospreypublishing.com
www.ospreypublishing.com

OSPREY is a trademark of Osprey Publishing Ltd

First published in Great Britain in 2018

A catalog record for this book is available from the British Library.

ISBN: PB 9781472820631; eBook 9781472820655;
ePDF 9781472820648; XML 9781472824202

18 19 20 21 22   10 9 8 7 6 5 4 3 2 1

Map by bounford.com
Index by Rob Munro
Typeset by PDQ Digital Media Solutions, Bungay, UK
Printed in Hong Kong through World Print Ltd.

Osprey Publishing supports the Woodland Trust, the UK's leading woodland
conservation charity. Between 2014 and 2018 our donations are being spent
on its Centenary Woods project in the UK.

To find out more about our authors and books visit
www.ospreypublishing.com. Here you will find extracts, author interviews,
details of forthcoming events and the option to sign up for our newsletter.

Acknowledgments
The author would like to thank David Rosenberg PhD and Osprey editor
Nick Reynolds for their significant assistance in getting this book completed.

Editor's note
US customary measurements, including US nautical miles, knots (kn), and
long tons, have been used in this book. For ease of comparison please refer to
the following conversion table:

1 nautical mile = 1.85km
1yd = 0.9m
1ft = 0.3m
1in = 2.54cm/25.4mm
1kn = 1.85km/h
1 long ton = 1.02 metric tonnes
1lb = 0.45kg

Cover art: On August 31, 1942, *I-26* was presented with a perfect opportunity
for a torpedo attack against the carrier *Saratoga*. The submarine came to
periscope depth and fired six torpedoes. One broached, four missed, but one
hit the carrier on the starboard side, causing enough damage to knock *Saratoga*
out of action for months. The destroyers *Phelps* and *MacDonough* – the latter
is shown here rushing toward the periscope of *I-26* – gained sonar contacts on
the submarine and mounted deliberate depth-charge attacks. *I-26* survived to
sink the light cruiser *Juneau* on November 13, 1942; the submarine also
accounted for nine Allied merchant ships during the war.

Title-page photograph: The USN destroyer *Hammann* is shown sinking by the
bow after being torpedoed by the IJN submarine *I-168* during the afternoon
of June 6, 1942. None of the six destroyers screening the crippled carrier
Yorktown detected *I-168* during the boat's approach, allowing the Japanese
skipper, Lieutenant Commander Tanabe Yahachi, to set up a perfect attack.
(80-G-32320 courtesy of the Naval History & Heritage Command)

Artist's note
Readers may care to note that the original paintings from which the color
plates in this book were prepared are available for private sale. All reproduction
copyright whatsoever is retained by the publishers. All inquiries should be
addressed to:

p.wright1@btinternet.com

The publishers regret that they can enter into no correspondence upon
this matter.

CONTENTS

INTRODUCTION

The key premise of Japanese naval strategy for all but the last year leading up to the Pacific War was that a decisive fleet engagement would be fought with the United States Navy (USN) in the Western Pacific. Because the Imperial Japanese Navy (IJN) was outnumbered by the USN, the Japanese planned to employ strong attritional tactics before the grand battle. The IJN saw its submarine force as a key part of this attritional strategy. Accordingly, the IJN became the leading proponent of large, long-range submarines suitable for conducting attritional attacks at extended ranges. In order to accomplish its mission, the IJN's submarine force was required to perform extended reconnaissance of the USN's battle fleet, even in port, and then shadow and attack it. This led to the IJN being the only navy to make extensive use of submarine-launched aircraft during World War II. In addition to submarines that could carry and launch aircraft, the IJN built a large number of cruiser submarines based on World War I German technology and even command submarines. The IJN expected much from its submarine force at the start of the Pacific War.

For its part, the USN was fully aware of the potential threat posed by Japanese submarines, though not of the specifics of the Japanese strategy to employ them. USN destroyers were equipped and trained to screen the battle fleet as it moved across the Pacific Ocean. However, the destroyers were always intended to be multi-mission platforms and their primary design focus was to enable them to act as surface-warfare platforms. Providing antiaircraft defense for themselves and the battle fleet was also a priority. While every USN destroyer was fitted and trained for antisubmarine warfare (ASW), this capability was not well developed by the start of the war, which made the USN's major fleet units potentially vulnerable to submarine attack.

When war in the Pacific broke out on December 7, 1941, the IJN had a total of 64 submarines in service. With this force, the IJN immediately attempted to execute its

strategy of focusing its submarine operations to attack USN major fleet units. The cream of the IJN's submarine force, 28 fleet submarines, were sent to Hawaii as part of the Pearl Harbor attack in order to finish off the crippled Pacific Fleet. Overall, results were very disappointing, but the IJN submarine *I-6* did succeed in torpedoing the carrier *Saratoga* on January 11, 1942, which forced the ship to miss the carrier battles of Coral Sea (May 4–8, 1942) and Midway (June 4–7, 1942). USN destroyers proved unable to protect *Saratoga*, and the only IJN submarine lost during what the Japanese termed the Hawaiian Operation (*I-70* on December 10, 1941) was sunk by carrier-based aircraft. The Hawaiian Operation was the first indication that the IJN's submarine employment strategy and submarine tactics were flawed, but this failure did not force an immediate change. During the Midway operation in June 1942, submarines were to play an important part in the IJN's plan for a decisive battle against the US Pacific Fleet, but they failed in their primary mission to detect and attack USN fleet units moving to support US forces on Midway Atoll. Though IJN submarines failed in this critical mission, one well-handled submarine (*I-168*) succeeded in sinking the already-crippled carrier *Yorktown* on June 7. Again, USN destroyers proved unable to protect major fleet units.

Despite a professed shift in priority from attacking naval targets to attacking merchant shipping, during the Guadalcanal campaign the IJN continued to link most of its submarine operations to attacking USN fleet units. The USN created the condition for this to pay off by operating in the same area for extended periods, thus allowing the IJN to deploy its submarines for maximum effect. For the only time in

I-3, shown here, was one of four Type J1 cruiser submarines. Note the two 5.5in deck guns. The number "8" on the bow denotes the submarine's parent submarine division. *I-3* was sunk by PT boats off Guadalcanal in December 1942 on a supply mission. (NH 55616 courtesy of the Naval History & Heritage Command)

the war, Japanese submarines played a major role when *I-26* damaged *Saratoga* again on August 31 and then *I-19* sank the carrier *Wasp* on September 15. The same salvo that sank *Wasp* also damaged the modern battleship *North Carolina* and sank the destroyer *O'Brien*, making it the most destructive single submarine torpedo salvo of the war. The heavy cruiser *Chester* was damaged by *I-176* on October 20, and the light cruiser *Juneau* was sunk by *I-26* on November 13. On none of these occasions did USN destroyers sink the attacking submarine. Concurrent with attacks on USN fleet units, IJN submarines were ordered to attack USN sea lines of communications (SLOCs) to Guadalcanal. In this endeavor, IJN submarines were totally ineffective as their passive tactics were unable to achieve results against defended supply lines.

Even as the Japanese were allocating their most capable and modern submarines to support major IJN operations, smaller groups of submarines were assigned missions not directly in support of specific fleet operations. Many of the submarines which supported the Pearl Harbor attack were later released to attack merchant shipping off the US West Coast, but the results were very disappointing. Older submarines were assigned to support the invasion of the Dutch East Indies and then subsequently sent into the Indian Ocean to act as commerce raiders. In the Indian Ocean, where Allied defenses were weak, IJN submarines did achieve good results, supporting the contention that they were potentially better employed in attacks against commerce. Meanwhile, IJN submarine commanders were distracted by a secret weapon, the midget submarine, which needed a "mother" submarine to transport it to the target area, and other submarines to find targets. These operations took several modern submarines out of the IJN's main operations and devoted them to spectacular attacks of little military value. The employment of midget submarines at Pearl Harbor was a complete failure, and follow-up attacks at Sydney, Australia and Diego Suarez on Madagascar resulted in little damage to Allied naval forces.

An even greater distraction to IJN submarine operations began in late 1942 when the IJN found it increasingly difficult to supply Japanese garrisons in the South Pacific in the face of the increasing weight of Allied air power. One of the few methods

available to supply isolated garrisons on Guadalcanal and later on New Guinea was by using submarines; but this was extremely inefficient given the load capacities of even large submarines and came at the high cost of removing the submarines from conventional operations. This became an increasing burden on the IJN's submarine force as more and more Japanese garrisons found themselves isolated as the war progressed. Eventually the IJN, and even the Imperial Japanese Army, designed a dedicated transport submarine to lessen the burden on fleet submarines.

The commonly accepted conclusion is that IJN submarines were ineffective in the first part of the Pacific War in their primary mission of attacking USN major fleet units. Nevertheless, IJN submarines did enjoy several important successes at little cost to themselves. This book will examine whether the common wisdom is true.

I-68 (later *I-168*) pictured underway in March 1934, probably during trials. On June 6, 1942, this submarine scored the IJN's biggest success during the Battle of Midway thanks to a brilliantly executed attack by the boat's skipper, Lieutenant Commander Tanabe Yahachi. (NH 73054 courtesy of the Naval History & Heritage Command)

This photo was taken from an accompanying destroyer and shows the carrier *Yorktown* sinking just after dawn on June 7, 1942. In the right foreground is the ship's forefoot. The carrier has capsized to port, showing the large hole made by two of *I-168*'s torpedoes. The destroyer *Monaghan* is in the distance. (NH 106003 courtesy of the Naval History & Heritage Command)

CHRONOLOGY

1926
March — The first of four Type J1 submarines is commissioned.

1927
March — The first of four Type KRS submarines and the first of nine Type KD3A/Type KD3B submarines are commissioned.

1929
April — The first of three Type KD4 submarines is commissioned.

1932
July — A single Type J1M submarine is commissioned.
December — The first of three Type KD5 submarines is commissioned.

1934
June — The first of eight Farragut-class destroyers is commissioned.
July — The first of eight Type KD6A/Type KD6B submarines is commissioned.

1935
May — A single Type J2 submarine is commissioned.
August — The first of eight Porter-class destroyer leaders is commissioned.

1936
November — The first of 18 Mahan-class destroyers is commissioned.

1937
March — The first of two Type J3 submarines is commissioned.

June — The first of four Gridley-class destroyers and the first of eight Bagley-class destroyers are commissioned.

1939
February — The first of ten Benham-class destroyers is commissioned.
August — The first of 12 Sims-class destroyers is commissioned.

1940
March — The first of five Type C1 submarines is commissioned.
June — The first of 24 Benson/Gleaves-class destroyers is commissioned.
September — The first of 20 Type B1 submarines is commissioned.

1941
February — The first of three Type A1 submarines is commissioned.

A single torpedo from IJN submarine *I-19* hit the battleship *North Carolina* on September 15, 1942. This photo, taken at Pearl Harbor Navy Yard, Hawaii, on October 11, 1942, shows the resulting damage. The blast of the Type 95 warhead created a large hole in the torpedo bulge below the armor belt. (NH 84439 courtesy of the Naval History & Heritage Command)

October	The first of 72 Bristol-class destroyers is commissioned.
December	30 I-boats are committed to support the Pearl Harbor attack; they sink no USN warships and only a handful of merchant ships.

1942

January	The IJN sends nine I-boats to the US West Coast to attack targets of opportunity; no USN ships are attacked or lost and only a handful of merchant ships are sunk.
January 11	*I-6* torpedoes the carrier *Saratoga* southwest of Pearl Harbor; the ship misses the carrier battles of Coral Sea and Midway.
March	IJN submarine employment strategy gives priority to attacking merchant ships over attacking USN warships.
May	Eight IJN submarines support the Japanese invasion of Port Moresby on New Guinea, but fail to sight a single USN ship.
June	14 IJN submarines support the invasion of Midway Atoll. They fail to spot the USN carriers moving to the area, but *I-168* sinks the crippled carrier *Yorktown* on June 7.
June	The first of 175 Fletcher-class destroyers is commissioned.
August	The first of ten Type KD7 submarines is commissioned.
August 7	The US landing on Guadalcanal in the Solomon Islands begins a six-month campaign.
August 24	The first IJN counterattack results in the Battle of the Eastern Solomons; 11 IJN submarines are deployed, but cannot attack a single USN fleet unit.
August 31	*I-26* torpedoes *Saratoga*; the carrier misses three months of the campaign.
September 15	In the single most deadly torpedo salvo of the war, *I-19* sinks the carrier *Wasp* and the destroyer *O'Brien*, and damages the battleship *North Carolina*.
October 20	*I-176* damages the heavy cruiser *Chester*.
November 13	*I-26* sinks the light cruiser *Juneau*.
November 16	The IJN orders fleet submarines to begin supplying the garrison on Guadalcanal.

Early IJN submarines, such as this Vickers C2 design, were derived from submarines procured from foreign sources. By 1928, Japan was fully capable of indigenous submarine design and construction. (NH 111773 courtesy of the Naval History & Heritage Command)

DESIGN AND DEVELOPMENT

IJN SUBMARINE STRATEGY AND DESIGN

From 1909 until 1940, the IJN refined a defensive naval strategy aimed at defeating the USN. The broad outline of this strategy assumed that the USN would mount an offensive from Hawaii to the west. As the USN fleet neared Japan, the IJN would orchestrate a decisive encounter between the respective battle fleets in the Western Pacific. Because the Washington Naval Treaty of 1922 set the IJN's battleship force tonnage at only 60 percent that of the USN battle fleet, a prerequisite for a successful decisive battle was the attrition of the advancing USN fleet. If the two battle fleets met on numerically even terms, the IJN could carry the day with its superior training and tactics.

The attrition strategy was known to the Japanese as "progressive reduction operations." At the outer edge of the strategy, the IJN envisioned the USN battle fleet being attacked by long-range submarines; and this requirement guided the design and development of almost all IJN prewar submarines and made the IJN the leading naval power for the development of large submarines. To perform their missions, these large submarines had to be able to conduct extended-range reconnaissance of the USN battle fleet (including while in port), pursue it, and then successfully attack it.

In order to conduct long-range interception and attack operations, each IJN submarine squadron had to have a flagship large enough to accommodate extensive communications facilities and with enough space to embark the squadron staff. The

Though not entirely successful, the IJN's first Type KD1 submarine proved that large submarines with a superior operating radius were practical. *I-51*, shown here, was decommissioned before the start of the war. (AirSeaLand Photos)

ship had to have a large steaming radius, fairly high speed, and enough defensive armament to deal with light USN surface forces. The notion that this mission was best fulfilled by a light cruiser persisted through 1937. In 1938, design work began on a new class of specially designed light cruisers to operate as submarine squadron flagships. The thinking was that such a ship would have all the attributes described above and the capability of carrying several fast, long-range floatplanes, which would spot targets for IJN submarines to attack. Eventually, one cruiser (*Ōyodo*) was completed to perform this mission, but when it finally entered service in early 1943 the purpose for which it had been designed was no longer practical, and the ship was converted into the Combined Fleet's flagship. Later, large command submarines replaced the light cruisers used as flagships because the submarines were obviously more likely to survive in enemy waters.

The first submarines in IJN service were five Holland-class boats built by the US firm Electric Boat Company and delivered in 1905. The Japanese duly copied this design to produce the first submarines built in Japan. (As was normal when the IJN delved into new technologies, the Japanese purchased the best foreign technology available and then sought to produce it in Japan as soon as possible.) The next

The Type KD2 boat *I-52* was based on Germany's World War I long-range cruiser submarines. Obsolete by the start of World War II, the submarine served as a training boat from 1940 and was decommissioned in July 1942. (NH 111798 courtesy of the Naval History & Heritage Command)

generation of IJN submarines was comprised of units bought from Britain and France, augmented by boats built in Japan under license from British and Italian companies. Japanese submarine technology was accelerated by the acquisition of seven German U-boats after World War I. These represented the state of the art for the period and formed the basis for the expansion of the IJN's submarine force. By 1928, with the help of several hundred German submarine designers, technicians, and former U-boat officers, the Japanese were self-reliant in the design and construction of submarines.

As mentioned above, the IJN wanted its submarines to be able to conduct long-range scouting and attack operations. This required large boats capable of high speed and with great endurance. After an unsuccessful attempt to build a large submarine based on a British design, the Japanese turned to using one of their U-boat prizes as an example. *U-139* was used as the basis for *kaidai* (abbreviated from *kaigun-dai* or large fleet type) Type 2 (KD2) launched in 1922. The Type KD2 was successful from a design perspective and served as a springboard for all IJN large fleet boats built up until the start of the Pacific War.

The Type KD2 boats were successful because of their high surface speed (22kn), long range (10,000 miles at 10kn), and heavy armament (eight 21in torpedo tubes and 16 torpedoes). By necessity, they were large boats, which gave them good seakeeping characteristics. All future IJN fleet submarine designs shared these basic characteristics. However, because Japan's intricate attrition strategy called for submarines to perform several tasks, it was evident that a single submarine design could not fulfill all these requirements, so several different designs were developed to specialize in different missions. The *junsen* or ocean-cruising submarine was intended for independent long-range operations. Type A boats were designed as command submarines to coordinate squadron operations. Type B boats were optimized for the scouting mission and thus were equipped with the facilities to carry and launch floatplanes. Type C boats were optimized for attack missions and thus were given additional torpedo tubes and a slightly higher speed.

The first *junsen* (Type J1) boats were delivered in 1927. These possessed an extraordinary range of 24,000 miles and an endurance of 60 days. Only four such boats were completed to this design, however, because they proved to be only a limited success. Their extra-long range proved of no particular value and their large hulls made them difficult to handle underwater and slow to dive. The single Type J1M boat, completed in 1932, was almost identical to the Type J1, but with one major difference: when delivered, it was the first Japanese submarine designed to carry a floatplane. The aircraft-handling facilities were removed in 1940, however, so the Type J1M boat was employed in similar fashion to the Type J1 boats. A single Type J2 boat was completed with the same awkward configuration as the Type J1M, placing the aircraft-handling facilities aft of the conning tower. The boat was built with more powerful diesel engines, which gave it a top surface speed of 20kn but lowered its range to 20,000 miles. The final *junsen* boats were the two Type J3 units. These were the largest IJN submarines built before the Pacific War and constituted the ultimate development of the cruiser concept. They retained the aircraft-handling facilities of the earlier *junsen* designs and their large size made them well suited as flagships, and they were used in this capacity for the first part of the war. In general, the Japanese did not view the cruiser submarines as being suited for attacks on enemy fleet units. Their large

operational radius meant they were better suited for operations such as long-range attacks on enemy bases and SLOCs.

The IJN developed and built different types of submarines concurrently. After the success of the single Type KD2 boat, the Japanese worked to perfect the *kaidai* design. In general, the *kaidai* boats had higher surface speeds, making them better suited for attacks on the enemy's main naval forces. The four Type KD3A boats could be distinguished from the five Type KD3B boats by their different bow shape and sail configuration. This design emphasized speed (20kn) and firepower (16 torpedoes and eight tubes), while still possessing great range (14,000 miles). By the start of the war, these boats were showing their age and the surviving seven were assigned to secondary areas before being shifted to training duties beginning in March 1942.

There were three Type KD4 boats. These were slightly smaller than the preceding *kaidai* design and carried two fewer torpedoes and tubes. The last two KD4 boats were delivered in 1930, so they too were obsolescent by the start of the war. The three Type KD5 submarines had the same dimensions and capabilities as the Type KD4 boats, but the newer design possessed greater structural strength, which meant they could dive deeper.

The next class, the six Type KD6A and two Type KD6B boats, maximized speed. These were fitted with more powerful diesel engines and had longer hulls, which gave them a maximum surface speed of 23kn – the highest of any submarine when they first entered service in 1934. The two Type KD6B boats were built with strengthened hulls, which increased their maximum diving depth to 278ft.

The ultimate expression of the *kaidai* type was the Type KD7. The first of the ten units in the class was delivered in August 1942. These boats were a repeat of the Type KD6, but with a smaller range and a reduction of the torpedo armament to six tubes and 12 torpedoes.

To direct the actions of a deployed submarine squadron, the IJN built specially designed command submarines, namely the Type A1 and Type A2. These were the first boats to be built with the command function in mind and were based on the Type J3 design, but had additional space for command staff and a larger communications suite. They were also equipped with aircraft-handling facilities that could accommodate a single floatplane, but the catapult and hangar were moved to the front of the boat; a much more efficient arrangement, which decreased launch and

This is Type C1 boat *I-16*, pictured before the war. Note the lack of aircraft-handling facilities and the shape of the sail, which is clearly based on that of the Type KD boats. (AirSeaLand Photos)

recovery times. The boats' larger size permitted extra fuel and provisions to be carried, thus extending patrol duration to up to 90 days. Two Type A1 boats were completed before the war, and a third was commissioned in May 1942. The sole Type A2 boat, which carried much less powerful diesel engines, did not enter service until 1944. Two more Type A2 boats were completed as Type AM aircraft-carrying submarines, but neither of them entered service before December 1944.

The largest IJN submarine class and arguably the most successful was the Type B1: 20 boats were eventually completed to this design, with 16 entering service before 1943. This class combined the functions of the *kaidai* and *junsen* concepts into a single hull. Powerful diesel engines drove the boats to a maximum speed of 23.5kn on the surface. Endurance remained high at 14,000 miles. Type B1 boats carried six torpedo tubes and a total of 17 torpedoes. To enhance its scouting capabilities, the class was equipped with an aircraft hangar and catapult forward; there was space in the hangar for a single floatplane. As will be described later, boats of this class were responsible for most of the successes achieved by the IJN's submarine force against USN fleet units. The IJN was satisfied with the performance of the Type B1 boats and continued to build modified versions through 1944. The six Type B2 boats, all of which were completed in 1943 or later, were virtual copies of the Type B1 design but carried less powerful diesel engines. Three Type B3 boats, equipped with even less powerful engines, were not completed until 1944.

The final type of fleet submarine brought into service by the IJN before the war was the Type C, designed as an attack boat and thus maximizing firepower. Each of the five boats in the class was built with two forward torpedo rooms with four tubes. A total of 20 torpedoes were carried. The boats retained a high surface speed of 23.5kn and a range of 14,000 miles. The five Type C1 boats were based on the Type KD6 design, but were more maneuverable. Probably for that reason, all five boats were selected for conversion into midget-sub carriers. This capability drove their operational assignments; all were employed as midget-sub mother ships at Pearl Harbor and were retained in this role for most of 1942. An additional three Type C2 boats did not enter service until 1944, and three Type C3 boats did not reach the IJN fleet until December 1943.

All of the boats described above were considered fleet units by the IJN. Accordingly, their fleet numbers were prefixed with I – the first Romanized letter in traditional

Japanese syllabary. RO (the second Romanized letter) boats were second-class submarines designed for coastal operations. Because RO boats did not conduct long-range patrols, they will not be considered in this book. In any event, only a small number of RO boats were available at the start of the war: of the 36 Type KS and Type K6 boats, only six had entered service by 1942.

The IJN also brought several classes of special-function submarines into service. Four Type KRS minelaying submarines were commissioned in 1927–28 and were employed during the first part of the war as minelayers or to refuel flying boats. The two survivors were assigned to training duties in 1943. To take the burden of resupply missions off the I-boats, the IJN built 13 Type D1 and Type D2 supply submarines, but these did not enter service until 1944. Perhaps the best-known Japanese submarine is the *Sen-Toku* (Special Submarine) type. The largest submarines built during the war by any navy, each was designed to carry three attack floatplanes, but none of the three boats completed before the war saw combat service.

The final result of the IJN's love for large submarines was the *Sen-Toku* (Special Submarine) type, the largest submarines completed by any nation during World War II. This is *I-402*, one of only three units actually completed before the end of the war. Despite their size, they could only carry three aircraft, which would have been totally inadequate in any attack on strategic targets in the United States – the original mission of the *Sen-Toku* type. (AirSeaLand Photos)

I-14 was one of two Type AM boats. These were based on the Type A2 design, but were modified during construction to carry two aircraft in recognition of the fact that the original command and scouting missions of the Type A submarines were no longer relevant. The extra aircraft was added to increase the class's strike capability, but the marginal strike potential of the Type AM made it a waste of resources when Japan should have been building a large number of smaller submarines. (AirSeaLand Photos)

USN DESTROYER STRATEGY AND DESIGN

The USN envisioned a key role for destroyers in any possible war with Japan. Much like the IJN, USN prewar strategy was formulated around a decisive naval engagement in the Western Pacific. In such a battle, all fleet arms had a role, but the ultimate decision would be forced by a duel of battleships. Within this construct, the primary mission of USN destroyers was to attack the IJN battle line. This required destroyers with a high speed, heavy torpedo armament, and a heavy gun battery to protect the destroyer from attacks by Japanese screening units as it closed for a torpedo attack. A corollary to the mission to attack IJN capital ships was the mission to screen USN battleships from similar attacks. Because the USN lacked adequate light cruisers for this mission, destroyers were expected to carry this burden.

The USN's destroyers had to be more than just good torpedo boats. The Americans expected the IJN's attritional attacks as the USN moved into the Western Pacific. Accordingly, destroyers had to be able to mount a dual-purpose battery with modern fire-control equipment to deal with Japanese air attacks mounted by land-based bombers flying from a web of island bases. These missions tended to overshadow the traditional mission of destroyers – screening the main fleet from submarine attack. To protect its battle fleet from submarine attack, the USN planned to employ destroyers and aircraft in ASW roles; but because ASW aircraft would not be available and in any case had limited loiter time, the bedrock of fleet antisubmarine defenses was a strong destroyer screen.

Given the multiple missions the USN expected its destroyers to perform, and given the range requirements of conducting a war in the Pacific, the Americans preferred to build large destroyers. Following the end of World War I, the USN was well supplied with three classes of 1,190-ton flush-deck destroyers. The last of these were commissioned in 1922. Even after the transfer of 50 flush-deckers to Great Britain in 1940, the USN still retained 120 in service. However, these ships were obsolescent going into the war, and had already been replaced by new units for fleet work.

The London Naval Treaty of 1930 placed limits on destroyer tonnage for all the major powers and dictated the maximum size of destroyers. This challenged designers to meet the competing requirements of armament, machinery capable of high speed, and large fuel reserves for endurance into a single hull. As already mentioned, American designers preferred larger ships and 1,500 tons was settled on as the optimum size for incorporating the desired capabilities with the desired numbers of destroyers attainable under the tonnage restrictions. The first ships laid down to a new design were the eight-ship Farragut class in 1932. The design was a great advance over the old destroyers then in service and provided a template for most USN destroyers built up until the start of the Pacific War. The class introduced the excellent 5in/38 dual-purpose gun along with world-class fire-control equipment, new high-pressure boilers which produced a very high maximum speed of 36.5kn, and enhanced seakeeping in part due to the incorporation of a raised forecastle. The ships carried five 5in/38 dual-purpose guns and eight 21in torpedo tubes in two quadruple launchers. For antisubmarine duties, the ships were equipped with a hull-mounted sonar and space was reserved for depth-charge racks in wartime. All eight ships saw action in the Pacific during the war, and three (*Worden*, *Hull*, and *Monaghan*) were lost in 1943–44.

Mahan maneuvers near another destroyer and a battleship during the Battle of the Santa Cruz Islands on October 26, 1942. *Mahan* was the lead ship in a class of 18 that saw extensive service in the South Pacific throughout 1942, including as ASW screening ships for carrier task forces. (80-G-30169 courtesy of the Naval History & Heritage Command)

Gridley, lead ship in a class of four, pictured at anchor prior to the start of the Pacific War. This class featured a 16-tube torpedo battery and only four 5in/38 single mounts, as can be seen in this view. (NH 67719 courtesy of the Naval History & Heritage Command)

Per the London Naval Treaty, 16 percent of destroyer tonnage could be built up to a maximum of 1,850 tons. The eight ships of the Porter class were laid down in 1933 to take advantage of the larger size. Designed as destroyer leaders, they provided space for an embarked staff; and their larger size also allowed for a larger main battery of four twin 5in/38 mounts (which were not dual purpose) and eight 21in torpedo tubes. The machinery featured an improved arrangement with separate engine and boiler rooms. Higher-pressure boilers and a longer hull brought the top speed up to 37kn. A hull-mounted sonar and stern-mounted depth-charge racks were fitted. Of the eight ships in the class, five served in the Pacific with one (*Porter*) being sunk by enemy action.

The USN's tonnage allotment for 1,850-ton destroyers translated to 13 such ships. To use this allotment, the five-ship Somers class was laid down beginning in 1935. However, because all five ships spent their entire careers in the Atlantic during the war, they will not be described here in detail.

The 18-ship Mahan class returned to the standard 1,500-ton size. The new class emphasized a heavier torpedo battery. An additional quadruple mount was added, but the arrangement of the three quadruple mounts permitted only an eight-torpedo broadside. Five single 5in/38 dual-purpose guns were retained even with the increased torpedo armament. The Mahan class also introduced a new generation of destroyer machinery which used higher-pressure boilers and lighter turbines. These proved more efficient and were highly reliable in service. This class was the best of the USN's 1,500-ton designs. All 18 ships served in the Pacific and six (*Mahan, Reid, Tucker, Cushing, Perkins,* and *Preston*) were eventually sunk in action.

The four-ship Gridley class further increased the torpedo battery by adding another quadruple torpedo bank, giving each ship a total of 16 torpedo tubes, eight on each beam. The 5in/38 battery was reduced to four in an effort to reduce topweight. The class was fitted with a new high-pressure boiler, which resulted in a top speed of 42.8kn for *Maury* during the ship's acceptance trials – the highest recorded speed for a USN destroyer. Nevertheless, stability problems created by excessive topweight and the lack of hull strength rendered the design a failure. All were withdrawn from Pacific operations before the end of the war.

The eight-ship Bagley class was laid down beginning in 1935. Externally, they were similar to the Gridley-class destroyers and retained the same heavy torpedo battery of 16 21in torpedo tubes and a reduced 5in/38 battery of four single guns. For machinery, the class reverted to that of the earlier Mahan class. Because they enjoyed increased stability compared to the Gridley class, the Bagley-class destroyers were considered successful. The entire class was very active in the Pacific with two (*Blue* and *Jarvis*) being sunk and four damaged during 1942 alone.

The ten ships of the Benham class, which began to enter service in 1939, were the last of the 1,500-ton designs. The ships retained the basic configuration first introduced in the Gridley class with the heavy torpedo battery of four quadruple launchers. The main-gun battery remained at four single 5in/38 mounts. By this time, the notion of fitting a heavy gun and torpedo battery on a 1,500-ton ship still capable of high speeds was proving increasingly difficult. The Benham class came in 10 percent overweight, but this was no longer an issue within treaty limitations because the Second London Naval Treaty of 1936 had removed the individual tonnage limit in favor of an overall tonnage limit. Six of these ships served in the Pacific during the early-war period with one (*Benham*) being sunk and another damaged.

Construction of the 12 ships of the Sims class began in 1937. Because this was after the expiration of the London Naval Treaty of 1930, designers were able to increase the ships' standard displacement to 1,764 tons. The extra tonnage was used to keep a five-gun 5in/38 battery and three quadruple torpedo mounts. When the first ships entered service, however, they were found to be seriously top-heavy which forced a reduction to two quadruple torpedo mounts and four 5in/38 mounts in service. Nine of this class were active early in the Pacific War and four (*Sims*, *Hammann*, *O'Brien*, and *Walke*) were lost.

The Sims class, the lead ship of which is shown here off Boston Navy Yard, Massachusetts, on May 9, 1940, reverted to the configuration with five 5in/38 single mounts and two quadruple torpedo mounts. *Sims* was lost on May 7, 1942 at the Battle of Coral Sea. (19-N-21805 courtesy of the Naval History & Heritage Command)

The ten-ship Benham class was essentially a repeat of the Gridley class. This is *Benham* pictured off Mare Island Navy Yard on February 6, 1942. *Benham* was sunk in a surface action off Guadalcanal on November 15, 1942. (NH 90936 courtesy of the Naval History & Heritage Command)

The most modern USN destroyers in commission at the start of the war were from the Benson/Gleaves class. These were laid down beginning in 1939 and were improved versions of the Sims class. Armament was intended to be the same three quadruple torpedo mounts and five 5in/38 guns as the Sims-class destroyers, but when commissioned, only two quintuple torpedo mounts were fitted. The machinery was arranged in two separate units, that is each with its own boiler and machinery room. This reduced the possibility that a single torpedo hit could cripple the ship's propulsion system. The separated machinery arrangement necessitated two stacks. Also for the first time, the emergency diesel generator was placed on the main deck where it would not be affected by flooding. Displacement of the new classes was slightly greater than that of the Sims class due to the greater weight of the machinery and some hull strengthening.

The initial ships in the 24-ship class were designed and built by two different shipbuilders, which accounts for the slight differences within the class. The first two ships (including *Benson*) were designed by Bethlehem Shipbuilding and given a different set of machinery from Bethlehem. The next two ships (including *Gleaves*) were designed by Gibbs and Cox and built by Bath Iron Works and were given new high-pressure steam plants. The two versions could be distinguished by their stacks; the Bath ships had round stacks and the Bethlehem ships, flattened stacks. Of the 24 ships, only four saw action in the Pacific. Of these, three were lost, including two (*Meredith* and *Monssen*) off Guadalcanal in 1942.

The Benson/Gleaves class was used as the basis for the next class – the 72-ship Bristol class. The immediate need for destroyers was apparent in late 1940, so construction of the Benson/Gleaves class was continued with little modification. The quintuple torpedo mounts were retained and almost all were completed to the four

5in/38 gun design. As originally designed, only ten depth charges were carried with two stern-mounted racks. Most of the class served in the Atlantic where ASW was their primary mission. On some of these ships, the after bank of torpedoes was removed in favor of up to 60 depth charges and six depth-charge projectors. Pacific Fleet units did not carry this heavy ASW fit. None of the ships in this class was completed before the outbreak of war in the Pacific and eventually only 24 found their way to the Pacific theater. Seven were active in the Pacific during 1942, with one (*Duncan*) being sunk in that year.

The final class of American destroyers to serve in the Pacific in 1942 was the Fletcher class. The Fletchers were much larger than previous destroyer designs with the result being a better-balanced design. The ships were fitted with powerful machinery, which generated a maximum speed of 38kn, a torpedo battery of two quintuple mounts, a main-gun battery of five 5in/38 mounts, and even some protective plating to key areas such as the bridge, command, and machinery areas. The ships were big enough to accept additional top weight in the form of a greatly expanded antiaircraft battery without sacrificing any of the torpedoes or 5in/38 mounts. All 175 of these ships were sent to the Pacific, and eventually 18 were lost in 1943–45.

The Fletchers were probably the best destroyers of World War II. This is the lead ship maneuvering off New York on July 18, 1942. Note the ASW suite of three K-guns per beam and two stern-mounted depth-charge racks. (19-N-31243 courtesy of the Naval History & Heritage Command)

THE STRATEGIC SITUATION

The IJN's submarine force had been developed and trained for a defensive battle. When Vice Admiral Yamamoto Isoroku took over the Combined Fleet in August 1939, he changed decades of preparation for an attritional defensive campaign to an offensive strategy featuring expansion in the South and Central Pacific. As an important element of the IJN's attritional strategy, the submarine force's long-range weapons gave it the potential to play a successful part in Yamamoto's new aggressive strategy. The centerpiece of the strategy was Yamamoto's plan to attack Pearl Harbor.

RIGHT

The Sims-class destroyer *O'Brien* photographed soon after completion in May 1940. The destroyer arrived in the Pacific in January 1942 and was assigned to screen the carrier *Hornet* during an operation to move reinforcements to Guadalcanal. On September 15, *O'Brien* was struck by a torpedo launched from *I-19*. The structural damage was sufficient to sink the destroyer on October 19 while returning to the United States. (NH 97787 courtesy of the Naval History & Heritage Command)

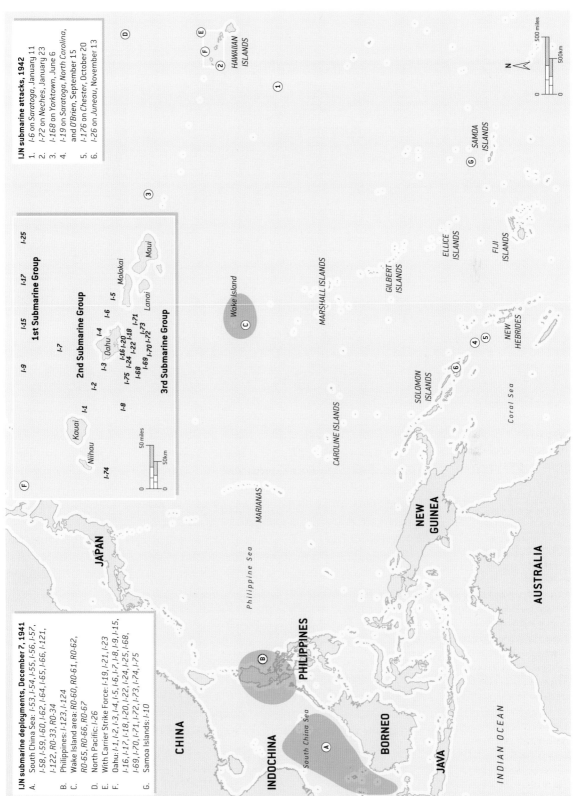

IJN submarine deployments, December 7, 1941

A. South China Sea: I-53, I-54, I-55, I-56, I-57, I-58, I-59, I-60, I-62, I-64, I-65, I-66, I-121, I-122, RO-33, RO-34

B. Philippines: I-123, I-124

C. Wake Island area: RO-60, RO-61, RO-62, RO-65, RO-66, RO-67

D. North Pacific: I-26

E. With Carrier Strike Force: I-19, I-21, I-23

F. Oahu: I-1, I-2, I-3, I-4, I-5, I-6, I-7, I-8, I-9, I-15, I-16, I-17, I-18, I-20, I-22, I-24, I-25, I-68, I-69, I-70, I-71, I-72, I-73, I-74, I-75

G. Samoa Islands: I-10

IJN submarine attacks, 1942

1. I-6 on *Saratoga*, January 11
2. I-72 on *Neches*, January 23
3. I-168 on *Yorktown*, June 6
4. I-19 on *Saratoga*, *North Carolina*, and *O'Brien*, September 15
5. I-176 on *Chester*, October 20
6. I-26 on *Juneau*, November 13

CHINA

JAPAN

INDOCHINA

PHILIPPINES

BORNEO

JAVA

NEW GUINEA

AUSTRALIA

South China Sea

Philippine Sea

MARIANAS

CAROLINE ISLANDS

MARSHALL ISLANDS

Wake Island

GILBERT ISLANDS

ELLICE ISLANDS

SOLOMON ISLANDS

NEW HEBRIDES

Coral Sea

FIJI ISLANDS

SAMOA ISLANDS

HAWAIIAN ISLANDS

INDIAN OCEAN

1st Submarine Group

2nd Submarine Group

3rd Submarine Group

Niihau

Kauai

Oahu

Molokai

Lanai

Maui

I-74

I-1

I-8

I-2

I-3

I-9

I-15

I-17

I-25

I-7

I-4

I-6

I-5

I-16

I-20

I-71

I-18

I-24

I-22

I-73

I-75

I-69

I-70

I-72

I-68

N

0 500km
0 500 miles

0 50km
0 50 miles

ABOVE LEFT

One of the IJN submarine force's greatest assets was the 21in Type 95 torpedo. It possessed a combination of a large warhead, high speed, and reliability. This is the torpedo room aboard a Japanese submarine. (AirSeaLand Photos)

ABOVE RIGHT

The IJN put great emphasis on submarine-launched aircraft; a capability that was deemed critical if IJN submarines were to carry out their mission of locating and attacking USN fleet units. In reality, this capability was only rarely used and then only to scout enemy bases. Here an E14Y1 "Glen" floatplane is being prepared for launch. Note the collapsible crane in the foreground; this was used to recover the aircraft. (AirSeaLand Photos)

To ensure the plan's success, and in line with the prewar emphasis on attacking USN fleet units, the Combined Fleet allocated its most modern fleet submarines to support the risky operation. The submarines retained a secondary mission to attack merchant shipping. This was aimed at vulnerable Allied SLOCs and would also serve to stretch Allied defenses. To conduct this secondary mission, nine of the submarines assigned to the Hawaiian Operation were ordered to proceed to the US West Coast after the Pearl Harbor attack.

Other Japanese offensive operations in the first phase of the war were supported by IJN submarines. The attack against British Malaya was allocated 16 submarines comprised of 12 old fleet boats, two minelaying boats, and two RO-type boats. Finally, the attack on Wake Island was allocated six old RO-type boats.

The USN was obviously caught off-guard by the attack on Pearl Harbor, the immediate result of which was to place the aircraft carrier decisively at the center of fleet operations. The USN's battle line was quickly rebuilt after the return of three lightly damaged battleships to service, all of which joined the Pacific Fleet's sole undamaged battleship, and the transfer of three more battleships from the Atlantic. Even so, the USN never employed these as front-line units, even during the initial period of the war when the USN was at its weakest. This was for a number of reasons, but the result was that these battleships did not operate in areas where they were likely to encounter IJN submarines.

This left the USN's carrier force to carry the burden of the war through 1942. Because the carriers were the centerpiece of the fleet, they became the primary targets

IJN SUBMARINE FORCE ORGANIZATION

The IJN's submarine force was broken down into a number of squadrons. The prescribed establishment for each squadron was three subordinate divisions each with three submarines. In 1940, as the result of a reorganization of the submarine force, a separate fleet was established and assigned the IJN's most modern submarines. The Sixth Fleet was comprised of three submarine squadrons and was assigned the mission of attacking USN fleet units. Other squadrons were assigned to other fleets and given older submarines to perform the missions specific to those fleets. Each squadron was assigned submarines of a particular type for ease of maintenance and for tactical uniformity.

IJN SUBMARINE FORCE, DECEMBER 7, 1941

Combined Fleet
4th Submarine Squadron (flagship light cruiser *Kinu*)
    18th Submarine Division (*I-53*, *I-54*, *I-55*)
    19th Submarine Division (*I-56*, *I-57*, *I-58*)
    21st Submarine Division (*RO-33*, *RO-34*)
5th Submarine Squadron (flagship light cruiser *Yura*)
    28th Submarine Division (*I-59*, *I-60*)
    29th Submarine Division (*I-62*, *I-64*)
    30th Submarine Division (*I-65*, *I-66*)

Third Fleet
6th Submarine Squadron
    9th Submarine Division (*I-123*, *I-124*)
    13th Submarine Division (*I-121*, *I-122*)

Fourth Fleet
    26th Submarine Division (*RO-60*, *RO-61*, *RO-62*)
    27th Submarine Division (*RO-65*, *RO-66*, *RO-67*)
    33rd Submarine Division (*RO-63*, *RO-64*, *RO-68*)

Sixth Fleet (Vice Admiral Shimizu Mitsumi on flagship light cruiser *Katori*)
1st Submarine Squadron (Rear Admiral Satō Tsutomu on flagship *I-9*)
    1st Submarine Division (*I-15*, *I-16*, *I-17*)
    2nd Submarine Division (*I-18*, *I-19*, *I-20*)
    3rd Submarine Division (*I-21*, *I-22*, *I-23*)
    4th Submarine Division (*I-24*, *I-25*, *I-26*)
2nd Submarine Squadron (Rear Admiral Yamazaki Shigeteru on flagships *I-7* and *I-10*)
    7th Submarine Division (*I-1*, *I-2*, *I-3*)
    8th Submarine Division (*I-4*, *I-5*, *I-6*)
3rd Submarine Squadron (Rear Admiral Miwa Shigeyoshi on flagship *I-8*)
    11th Submarine Division (*I-74*, *I-75*)
    12th Submarine Division (*I-68*, *I-69*, *I-70*)
    20th Submarine Division (*I-71*, *I-72*, *I-73*)

Kure Naval District Force (*I-52*, *RO-31*)
    6th Submarine Division (*RO-57*, *RO-58*, *RO-59*)

of the IJN's submarine force; and because they were so few in number, the sinking or damaging of only one or two by IJN submarines could make an important, even a potentially decisive, contribution. The USN's Pacific Fleet began the war with only three carriers – the converted battlecruisers *Lexington* and *Saratoga*, and *Enterprise*. Three more joined during 1942: *Yorktown* was the first to move over from the Atlantic in December 1941; the new *Hornet* joined the fleet in mid-March 1942; and *Wasp* transferred to the Pacific in June 1942.

The USN proved just as aggressive as the IJN in the opening months of the war despite being outnumbered in all categories of combatants, including carriers. Carrier air raids were conducted against Japanese bases in the Central Pacific into February 1942, and against Japanese invasion forces in the South Pacific. When the IJN returned its full attention to expansion in the South Pacific in May 1942, to be followed by a massive operation against Midway Atoll in June, the IJN's submarine force faced the challenge of successfully attacking major USN fleet units.

TECHNICAL SPECIFICATIONS

IJN SUBMARINE CLASSES ACTIVE IN 1941–42

Based on the German Type UE II U-boats from World War I, the Type KRS minelaying submarines entered service in 1927–28. In 1940, all four boats in the class were fitted with aviation fuel tanks to enable them to refuel flying boats.

Type KRS specifications	
Units in class	I-121, I-122, I-123, I-124
Displacement	1,383 tons surfaced; 1,768 tons submerged
Dimensions	Length 279ft 6in; beam 24ft 6in; draft 14ft 6in
Machinery	Two diesels with 2,400shp driving two shafts; electric motors with 1,100shp
Speed	14.5kn surfaced; 7kn submerged
Range	10,500 miles at 8kn surfaced; 40 miles at 4.5kn submerged
Armament	Four 21in bow torpedo tubes; 12 torpedoes; one 5.5in deck gun; up to 42 mines could be carried in two mine shafts fitted aft of the sail
Operating depth	200ft
Crew	75

The four Type J1 boats, commissioned in 1926–29, were the IJN's first *junsen* (cruiser) submarines. Their large hulls were excellent for surface operations, but greatly increased diving time and gave the boats limited maneuverability when submerged. Overall, the class proved to be a limited success in its role as long-range attack boats. In late 1942, two boats (*I-1* and *I-2*) were modified as transports with the removal of the aft 5.5in gun, a reduction in the number of torpedo reloads, and provisions for carrying a 46ft landing craft or cargo rafts.

Type J1 specifications	
Units in class	*I-1, I-2, I-3, I-4*
Displacement	2,135 tons surfaced; 2,791 tons submerged
Dimensions	Length 320ft; beam 30ft 3in; draft 16ft 6in
Machinery	Two diesels with 6,000shp driving two shafts; electric motors with 2,600shp
Speed	18kn surfaced; 8kn submerged
Range	24,000 miles at 10kn surfaced; 60 miles at 3kn submerged
Armament	Six 21in torpedo tubes (four bow, two stern); 20 torpedoes; two 5.5in deck guns
Operating depth	265ft
Crew	68

The single Type J1M boat, completed in 1932, was nearly identical to the preceding Type J1 boats, but was the first Japanese submarine designed and fitted with provisions to handle an aircraft. The aircraft components were stored in two watertight cylinders fitted aft of the sail along with the catapult. This arrangement was a failure because excessive time was required to assemble the aircraft. By 1940, the aircraft-handling equipment was replaced by a second 5.5in deck gun.

Type J1M specifications	
Units in class	*I-5*
Displacement	2,243 tons surfaced; 2,921 tons submerged
Dimensions	Length 320ft; beam 30ft 3in; draft 16ft 6in
Machinery	Two diesels with 6,000shp driving two shafts; electric motors with 2,600shp
Speed	18kn surfaced; 8kn submerged
Range	24,000 miles at 10kn surfaced; 60 miles at 3kn submerged
Armament	Six 21in bow torpedo tubes; 20 torpedoes; two 5.5in deck guns
Operating depth	260ft
Crew	80

Commissioned in 1935, the single Type J2 boat shared the same awkward aircraft-handling arrangement as the Type J1M, but was fitted with more powerful diesel engines for a higher surface speed at the expense of range.

Type J2 specifications

Units in class	*I-6*
Displacement	2,243 tons surfaced; 3,061 tons submerged
Dimensions	Length 323ft; beam 29ft 9in; draft 17ft 6in
Machinery	Two diesels with 8,000shp driving two shafts; electric motors with 2,600shp
Speed	20kn surfaced; 7.5kn submerged
Range	20,000 miles at 10kn surfaced; 60 miles at 3kn submerged
Armament	Six 21in torpedo tubes (four bow, two stern); 17 torpedoes; one 5.5in deck gun; one 13mm machine gun; one floatplane
Operating depth	265ft
Crew	80

Commissioned in 1937 and 1938, the two Type J3 boats were the IJN's largest submarines before the war and represented the ultimate development of the cruiser-type design. In addition to retaining aircraft-handling facilities, they were large enough to serve as command platforms for squadron commanders.

Type J3 specifications

Units in class	*I-7, I-8*
Displacement	2,525 tons surfaced; 3,583 tons submerged
Dimensions	Length 358ft 6in; beam 29ft 9in; draft 17ft 3in
Machinery	Two diesels with 11,200shp driving two shafts; electric motors with 2,800shp
Speed	23kn surfaced; 8kn submerged
Range	14,000 miles at 16kn surfaced; 60 miles at 3kn submerged
Armament	Six 21in bow torpedo tubes; 20 torpedoes; one 5.5in deck gun, one single and two twin 13mm machine guns; one floatplane
Operating depth	330ft
Crew	80

The Type J3 submarines *I-7* and *I-8* were the largest IJN submarines before the war and acted as flagships for IJN submarine operations early in the conflict. On June 22, 1943, *I-7* was scuttled by its crew after being damaged by gunfire from the destroyer *Monaghan* off Kiska in the Aleutians. (AirSeaLand Photos)

The four Type KD3A and five Type KD3B boats were commissioned during 1927–30. The Type KD3A boats differed from the Type KD3B boats by virtue of the shape of their bow and the configuration of their sail. No aircraft-handling facilities were fitted. By the start of the war, these boats were nearing the end of their service lives and the surviving examples (*I-53* to *I-59*) were assigned to training duties from March 1942.

I-55, shown here, was one of nine Type KD3 submarines. These boats were obsolescent by the beginning of the war, so were employed in secondary areas. *I-55* sank two merchant ships in the Dutch East Indies before being assigned to training duties, and survived the war. (NH 111797 courtesy of the Naval History & Heritage Command)

Type KD3A/Type KD3B specifications	
Units in class	*I-53* (later *I-153*), *I-54* (later *I-154*), *I-55* (later *I-155*), *I-56* (later *I-156*), *I-57* (later *I-157*), *I-58* (later *I-158*), *I-59* (later *I-159*), *I-60*, *I-63*
Displacement	1,800 tons surfaced; 2,300 tons submerged
Dimensions	Length 330ft (*I-56*, *I-57*, *I-59*, *I-60*, *I-63*: 331ft 4in); beam 26ft; draft 15ft 9in (*I-56*, *I-57*, *I-59*, *I-60*, *I-63*: 16ft)
Machinery	Two diesels with 6,800shp driving two shafts; electric motors with 1,800shp
Speed	20kn surfaced; 8kn submerged
Range	10,000 miles at 10kn surfaced; 90 miles at 3kn submerged
Armament	Eight 21in bow torpedo tubes; 16 torpedoes; one 4.7in deck gun
Operating depth	200ft
Crew	60

Completed in 1929–30, the Type KD4 boats were slightly smaller than the Type KD3A and Type KD3B boats, but in most other respects were similar.

Type KD4 specifications

Units in class	I-61, I-62 (later I-162), I-64 (later I-164)
Displacement	1,720 tons surfaced; 2,300 tons submerged
Dimensions	Length 320ft 6in; beam 25ft 6in; draft 15ft 9in
Machinery	Two diesels with 6,000shp driving two shafts; electric motors with 1,800shp
Speed	20kn surfaced; 8.5kn submerged
Range	10,800 miles at 10kn surfaced; 60 miles at 3kn submerged
Armament	Six 21in torpedo tubes (four bow, two stern); 14 torpedoes; one 4.7in deck gun
Operating depth	200ft
Crew	60

Completed in 1932, the three Type KD5 boats were strengthened versions of the Type KD4. *I-67* was lost before the war.

Type KD5 specifications

Units in class	I-65 (later I-165), I-66 (later I-166), I-67
Displacement	1,705 tons surfaced; 2,330 tons submerged
Dimensions	Length 320ft 6in; beam 26ft 9in; draft 15ft 6in
Machinery	Two diesels with 6,000shp driving two shafts; electric motors with 1,800shp
Speed	20.5kn surfaced; 8.25kn submerged
Range	10,000 miles at 10kn surfaced; 60 miles at 3kn submerged
Armament	Six 21in bow torpedo tubes; 14 torpedoes; one 3.9in deck gun; one 13mm machine gun
Operating depth	230ft
Crew	75

Completed during 1934–38, the eight Type KD6A/Type KD6B boats were fitted with more powerful diesel engines for greater surface speed. The Type KD6B variant featured a strengthened hull, permitting a greater operating depth.

Type KD6A/Type KD6B specifications

Units in class	KD6A: I-68 (later I-168), I-69 (later I-169), I-70, I-71 (later I-171), I-72 (later I-172), I-73; KD6B: I-74 (later I-174), I-75 (later I-175)
Displacement	1,785 tons surfaced; 2,440 tons submerged
Dimensions	Length 343ft 6in (KD6B: 344ft 6in); beam 27ft; draft 15ft
Machinery	Two diesels with 9,000shp driving two shafts; electric motors with 1,800shp
Speed	23kn surfaced; 8.25kn submerged

Range	14,000 miles at 10kn surfaced (KD6B: 10,000 miles at 16kn); 65 miles at 3kn submerged
Armament	Six 21in bow torpedo tubes; 14 torpedoes; one 4.7in deck gun (*I-168*, *I-169*, *I-70*: one 3.9in deck gun); one 13mm machine gun (*I-174* and *I-175* mounted two)
Operating depth	245ft (KD6B: 278ft)
Crew	70

The final development of the *kaidai* (large fleet) type, the ten Type KD7 boats were essentially repeats of the Type KD6 with less surface range. The first boat did not enter service until August 1942 and the last was not completed until September 1943.

Type KD7 specifications	
Units in class	*I-76*, *I-77*, *I-78*, *I-79*, *I-80*, *I-81*, *I-82*, *I-83*, *I-84*, *I-85* (later *I-176* to *I-185*)
Displacement	1,833 tons surfaced; 2,602 tons submerged
Dimensions	Length 346ft; beam 27ft; draft 15ft
Machinery	Two diesels with 8,000shp driving two shafts; electric motors with 1,800shp
Speed	23kn surfaced; 8kn submerged
Range	8,000 miles at 16kn surfaced; 50 miles at 5kn submerged
Armament	Six 21in bow torpedo tubes; 12 torpedoes; one 4.7in deck gun; one twin 25mm antiaircraft gun
Operating depth	265ft
Crew	86

Designed as command boats to coordinate submarine squadron operations, the Type A1 boats had aircraft-handling facilities forward of the sail, thereby reducing the time required to launch, recover, and stow the aircraft. The first two boats entered service in 1941 and *I-11* in May 1942.

Type A1 specifications	
Units in class	*I-9*, *I-10*, *I-11*
Displacement	2,919 tons surfaced; 4,149 tons submerged
Dimensions	Length 372ft 9in; beam 31ft 4in; draft 17ft 6in
Machinery	Two diesels with 12,400shp driving two shafts; electric motors with 2,400shp
Speed	23.5kn surfaced; 8kn submerged
Range	16,000 miles at 16kn surfaced; 90 miles at 3kn submerged
Armament	Six 21in bow torpedo tubes; 18 torpedoes; one 5.5in deck gun; two twin 25mm antiaircraft guns; one floatplane
Operating depth	330ft
Crew	100

I-26

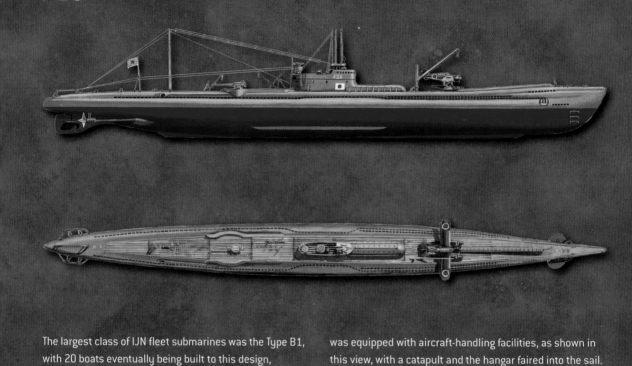

The largest class of IJN fleet submarines was the Type B1, with 20 boats eventually being built to this design, including some of the IJN's most successful units. The class was equipped with aircraft-handling facilities, as shown in this view, with a catapult and the hangar faired into the sail. *I-26*, shown here, carries an E14Y1 "Glen" floatplane.

Commissioned between 1940 and 1943, the Type B1 boats formed the IJN's most numerous class of fleet submarines. The design was based on the Type KD6, but with the addition of the same aircraft-handling facilities found on the Type A1.

Type B1 specifications

Units in class	*I-15, I-17, I-19, I-21, I-23, I-25, I-26, I-27, I-28, I-29, I-30, I-31, I-32, I-33, I-34, I-35, I-36, I-37, I-38, I-39*
Displacement	2,584 tons surfaced; 3,654 tons submerged
Dimensions	Length 356ft 6in; beam 30ft 6in; draft 16ft 9in
Machinery	Two diesels with 12,400shp driving two shafts; electric motors with 2,000shp
Speed	23.5kn surfaced; 8kn submerged
Range	14,000 miles at 16kn surfaced; 96 miles at 3kn submerged
Armament	Six 21in bow torpedo tubes; 17 torpedoes; one 5.5in deck gun; one twin 25mm antiaircraft gun; one floatplane
Operating depth	330ft
Crew	94

I-16

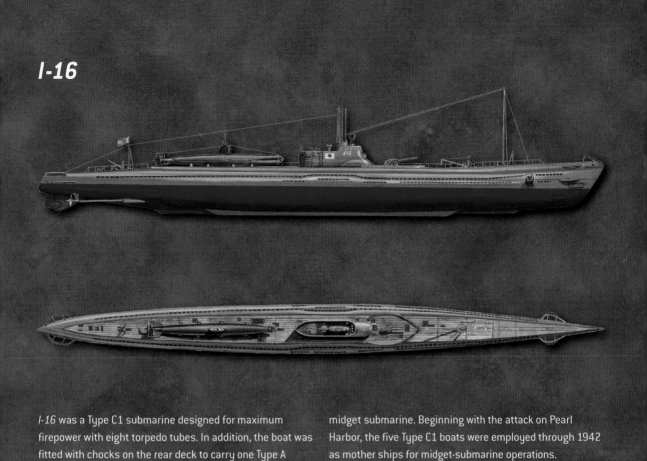

I-16 was a Type C1 submarine designed for maximum firepower with eight torpedo tubes. In addition, the boat was fitted with chocks on the rear deck to carry one Type A midget submarine. Beginning with the attack on Pearl Harbor, the five Type C1 boats were employed through 1942 as mother ships for midget-submarine operations.

Commissioned between March 1940 and October 1941, the five Type C1 boats were designed for maximum firepower and featured eight forward torpedo tubes in two separate torpedo rooms. The boats were also known for their maneuverability.

Type C1 specifications	
Units in class	*I-16, I-18, I-20, I-22, I-24*
Displacement	2,554 tons surfaced; 3,561 tons submerged
Dimensions	Length 358ft 6in; beam 30ft; draft 17ft 6in
Machinery	Two diesels with 12,400shp driving two shafts; electric motors with 2,000shp
Speed	23.5kn surfaced; 8kn submerged
Range	14,000 miles at 16kn surfaced; 60 miles at 3kn submerged
Armament	Eight 21in bow torpedo tubes; 20 torpedoes; one 5.5in deck gun; one twin 25mm antiaircraft gun; fittings to carry one Type A midget submarine
Operating depth	330ft
Crew	95

WORDEN

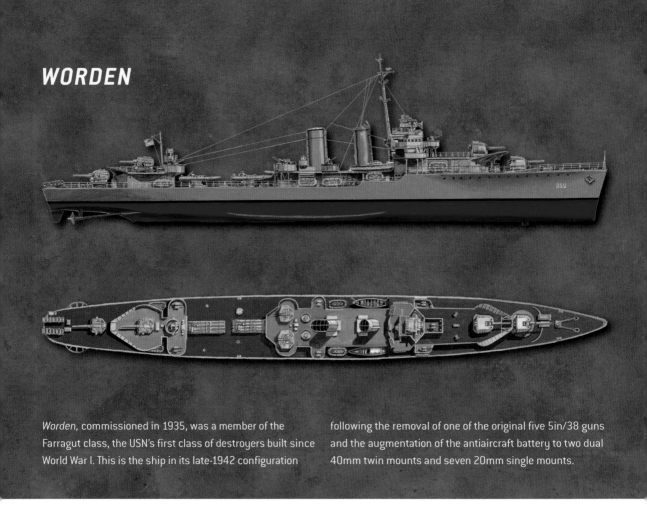

Worden, commissioned in 1935, was a member of the Farragut class, the USN's first class of destroyers built since World War I. This is the ship in its late-1942 configuration following the removal of one of the original five 5in/38 guns and the augmentation of the antiaircraft battery to two dual 40mm twin mounts and seven 20mm single mounts.

USN DESTROYER CLASSES ACTIVE IN 1941–42

The eight-ship Farragut class was the first American destroyer class built since 1921 and set the template for future prewar American destroyer designs. It featured a heavy gun and torpedo armament with a minimum of ASW weaponry.

Farragut-class specifications	
Units in class	*Farragut, Dewey, Hull, MacDonough, Worden, Dale, Monaghan, Aylwin*
Displacement	1,395 tons standard; 2,335 tons full load (variable among ships in the class)
Dimensions	Length 341ft 3in; beam 34ft 3in; draft 8ft 10in
Machinery	Four boilers; geared turbines on two shafts developing 42,800shp
Speed	36.5kn
Range	5,800 miles at 15kn
Armament (as completed)	Eight 21in torpedo tubes; five 5in/38 single mounts; four .5in machine guns; depth charges
Crew	250

FANNING

The 18 Mahan-class ships were staples in the ASW screens for USN task forces during the initial period of the Pacific War. Note that this class was fitted with a third bank of 21in torpedoes. This is *Fanning* in late 1942 following the removal of the No. 3 5in/38 gun and the addition of seven 20mm single mounts.

Designed as destroyer leaders, the Porter class ships used the maximum tonnage allowed by the London Naval Treaty of 1930 – 1,850 tons – giving them additional space for an embarked staff. The main-gun battery was fitted in four twin mounts, the heaviest on a USN destroyer.

Porter-class specifications	
Units in class	*Porter, Selfridge, McDougal, Winslow, Phelps, Clark, Moffett, Balch*
Displacement	1,834 tons standard; 2,597 tons full load
Dimensions	Length 381ft 1in; beam 37ft; draft 13ft
Machinery	Four boilers; geared turbines on two shafts developing 50,000shp
Speed	37kn
Range	6,500 miles at 12kn
Armament (as completed)	Eight 21in torpedo tubes; four 5in/38 twin mounts; two quadruple 1.1in mounts; two .5in machine guns; depth charges
Crew	194

The 18-ship Mahan class was the best American 1,500-ton destroyer design. It featured a heavy torpedo battery of 12 tubes in three quadruple mounts while keeping a five-gun main battery. It also introduced a new and very successful high-pressure steam plant.

Mahan-class specifications	
Units in class	Mahan, Cummings, Drayton, Lamson, Flusser, Reid, Case, Conyngham, Cassin, Shaw, Tucker, Downes, Cushing, Perkins, Smith, Preston, Dunlap, Fanning
Displacement	1,488 tons standard; 2,103 tons full load
Dimensions	Length 341ft 4in; beam 35ft 5in; draft 12ft 4in
Machinery	Four boilers; geared turbines on two shafts developing 49,000shp
Speed	36.5kn
Range	6,500 miles at 12kn
Armament (as completed)	12 21in torpedo tubes; five 5in/38 single mounts; four .5in machine guns; depth charges
Crew	158

The four-ship Gridley class maximized torpedo firepower with the addition of another quadruple bank for a total of 16 tubes. This was thought necessary by American designers because it would be impossible to replenish torpedoes during a fleet engagement.

Gridley-class specifications	
Units in class	Gridley, Craven, McCall, Maury
Displacement	1,590 tons standard; 2,219 tons full load
Dimensions	Length 340ft 10in; beam 35ft 10in; draft 12ft 9in
Machinery	Four boilers; geared turbines on two shafts developing 50,000shp
Speed	38.5kn
Range	6,500 miles at 12kn
Armament (as completed)	16 21in torpedo tubes; four 5in/38 single mounts; four .5in machine guns; depth charges
Crew	158

The eight-ship Bagley class was externally similar to the Gridley class, but was fitted with the machinery from the Mahan class. It kept the same heavy torpedo battery as the Gridley class, but possessed greater stability.

Bagley-class specifications	
Units in class	Bagley, Blue, Helm, Mugford, Ralph Talbot, Henley, Patterson, Jarvis
Displacement	1,646 tons standard; 2,245 tons full load
Dimensions	Length 341ft 4in; beam 35ft 6in; draft 12ft 10in

Machinery	Four boilers; geared turbines on two shafts developing 49,000shp
Speed	38.5kn
Range	6,500 miles at 12kn
Armament (as completed)	16 21in torpedo tubes; four 5in/38 single mounts; four .5in machine guns; depth charges
Crew	158

Because construction of the 12-ship Sims class began in 1937, after the Second London Naval Treaty of 1936, which removed the tonnage limit on individual ships, this class was heavier and larger than preceding designs. Nevertheless, these ships proved very top-heavy, requiring weight-saving measures that were incorporated into some ships while still under construction.

Sims-class specifications	
Units in class	*Sims, Hughes, Anderson, Hammann, Mustin, Russell, O'Brien, Walke, Morris, Roe, Wainwright, Buck*
Displacement	1,764 tons standard; 2,350 tons full load
Dimensions	Length 348ft 4in; beam 36ft; draft 12ft 10in
Machinery	Three boilers; geared turbines on two shafts developing 50,000shp
Speed	35kn
Range	6,500 miles at 12kn
Armament (as completed)	Eight 21in torpedo tubes; five 5in/38 single mounts; four .5in machine guns; depth charges
Crew	192

The ten-ship Benham class used the same hull lines and arrangement as the Gridley class. Its heavy gun and torpedo armament made the class overweight.

Benham-class specifications	
Units in class	*Benham, Ellet, Lang, Mayrant, Trippe, Rhind, Rowan, Stack, Sterett, Wilson*
Displacement	1,637 tons standard; 2,250 tons full load
Dimensions	Length 340ft 9in; beam 35ft 6in; draft 12ft 10in
Machinery	Three boilers; geared turbines on two shafts developing 50,000shp
Speed	38.5kn
Range	6,500 miles at 12kn
Armament (as completed)	16 21in torpedo tubes; four 5in/38 single mounts; four .5in machine guns; depth charges
Crew	184

All 24 ships of the Benson/Gleaves class were commissioned before the war, but only four served in the Pacific. The arrangements of the machinery spaces were altered

The 24-ship Benson/Gleaves class was originally fitted with five 5in/38 guns and two quadruple torpedo mounts, but despite the class's increased displacement, the ships were still considered top-heavy. This is *Benson*, pictured on May 10, 1943. Note that one of the torpedo mounts has been removed to address the topweight problem. The typical ASW suite of two stern-mounted depth-charge racks and six K-guns is also evident. (NH 80562 courtesy of the Naval History & Heritage Command)

to improve survivability; and two quintuple torpedo mounts were adopted and fitted on the centerline for the first time. The ASW armament was originally limited to two stern-mounted depth-charge racks. In 1941, a Y-gun was added, and in 1942, the ASW fit was increased to two depth-charge racks and six K-guns.

Benson/Gleaves-class specifications	
Units in class	*Gwin*, *Meredith*, *Grayson*, and *Monssen* served in the Pacific
Displacement	1,839 tons standard; 2,395 tons full load
Dimensions	Length 348ft 4in; beam 36ft 1in; draft 13ft 2in
Machinery	Four boilers; geared turbines on two shafts developing 50,000shp
Speed	35kn
Range	6,500 miles at 12kn
Armament (as completed)	Ten 21in torpedo tubes; five 5in/38in single mounts; six .5in machine guns; depth charges
Crew	208

The Bristol class was a repeat of the Benson/Gleaves class to meet the requirement for large numbers of destroyers as the USN geared up for war. Most of the 72 ships were built in a configuration featuring four 5in/38 guns and five torpedo tubes. This is *Laffey* at Espiritu Santo, New Hebrides, with survivors of the carrier *Wasp* on board. The light cruiser in the background is *Helena*. *Laffey* was sunk by the IJN battleship *Hiei* on November 13, 1942 off Guadalcanal. (NH 97865 courtesy of the Naval History & Heritage Command)

Driven by the need to build destroyers quickly in the period immediately before the war, the 72-ship Bristol class was essentially a repeat of the Benson/Gleaves class with slight modification.

Bristol-class specifications	
Units in class	*Laffey, Woodworth, Aaron Ward, Buchanan, Duncan, Lansdowne, Lardner, McCalla, Farenholt, Bailey, Bancroft, Barton, Meade, Caldwell, Coghlan, Frazier, Gansevoort, Gillespie, Kalk, Edwards, Welles, Stevenson, Stockton,* and *Thorn* served in the Pacific
Displacement	1,839 tons standard; 2,395 tons full load
Dimensions	Length 348ft 4in; beam 36ft 1in; draft 13ft 2in
Machinery	Four boilers; geared turbines on two shafts developing 50,000shp
Speed	35kn
Range	6,500 miles at 12kn
Armament (as completed)	Ten 21in torpedo tubes; four 5in/38 single mounts; one quadruple 1.1in mount; 4–6 20mm single mounts; depth charges
Crew	208

The Fletcher class was the first class of American destroyer built completely free of treaty restrictions and its design took advantage of wartime lessons. The first ship was not ordered until mid-1940, and the first of the type did not reach the Pacific until late 1942. The ship was much bigger than previous destroyer designs and therefore was fitted with machinery for a high maximum speed (38kn), a strong gun and torpedo armament, and even some protective plating to key areas such as the bridge, command, and machinery areas. The main-gun battery, five 5in/38 single mounts, was able to conduct dual-purpose fire guided by the excellent Mark 37 director. Another important improvement over earlier destroyer designs was the ability to accept additional antiaircraft guns without sacrificing any of the 5in/38 mounts or torpedoes. Torpedo armament was two quintuple mounts with no reloads. These were easily the best American destroyers of the war and possessed a fine balance of speed with offensive and defensive capabilities.

Fletcher-class specifications	
Units in class	All 175 served in the Pacific
Displacement	2,325 tons standard; 2,924 tons full load
Dimensions	Length 376ft 6in; beam 39ft 7in; draft 13ft 9in
Machinery	Four boilers; geared turbines on two shafts developing 60,000shp
Speed	38kn
Range	6,500 miles at 15kn
Armament (early war, as completed)	Ten 21in torpedo tubes; five 5in/38 single mounts; one quadruple 1.1in mount; four 20mm single mounts; two depth-charge racks, six K-guns
Crew	273

IJN SUBMARINE WEAPONS

Contrary to popular belief, Japanese submarines did not carry the renowned Type 93 (later known as the Long Lance) oxygen-propelled torpedo found on the IJN's surface ships. However, the most modern IJN submarine torpedo, the Type 95, was superb in its own right. It had a kerosene-oxygen wet-heater engine which gave it a long range and which ran largely trackless. It was also a reliable weapon, unlike USN submarine torpedoes of the period. The IJN also used several types of older torpedoes, with the Type 89 being the most numerous and important. It was propelled by a mix of kerosene and compressed air and was reliable in service.

Principal IJN submarine torpedoes		
Weapon	Warhead	Range
21in Type 95	891lb	9,850yd at 49–51kn; 13,100yd at 45–47kn
21in Type 89	661lb	6,000yd at 45kn; 6,550yd at 43kn; 10,900yd at 35kn

All I-boats carried some sort of deck gun. These were useful only as a last-ditch self-defense measure against much more heavily armed American destroyers, and were carried primarily for use against merchant ships. Against unescorted merchant ships, the standard tactic for I-boats was to conduct a "battle surface" and engage the merchant ship with deck guns to avoid expending a torpedo. The 5.5in/40 deck gun fitted to most IJN submarines had a maximum rate of fire of six rounds per minute. Also fitted on older IJN destroyers, the 4.7in/45 deck gun had a maximum rate of fire of five rounds per minute. The 3.9in/50 deck gun could also be used to engage aerial targets; its maximum rate of fire was six rounds per minute.

IJN submarine deck guns			
Weapon	Maximum range	Shell weight	Mounted on
5.5in/40 11th Year Type	17,500yd	83.8lb	J1, J1M, J2, J3, KRS, A1, B1, C1
4.7in/45 11th Year Type	17,500yd	45lb	KD3A, KD3B, KD4, KD7
3.9in/50 Type 88	17,700yd	28.7lb	KD6A, KD6B

IJN submarines were crippled by their lack of radar during the first period of the war. Not until 1944 did Japanese submarines receive radar, and it was inferior to American equipment. The lack of radar meant that the submarines were vulnerable to surprise attack by Allied ships and aircraft – a crucial vulnerability because the diving time for the large I-boats was already excessive. It also meant that in a scouting role IJN submarines were only as effective as the prowess of their lookouts, because use of a boat's fragile E14Y1 "Glen" floatplane was reserved for conducting reconnaissance of strategic targets, such as enemy bases.

The Type 88 was the mine laid by Type KRS boats. It was a copy of a World War I-era German contact mine with a 397lb charge.

IJN SUBMARINE ARMAMENT

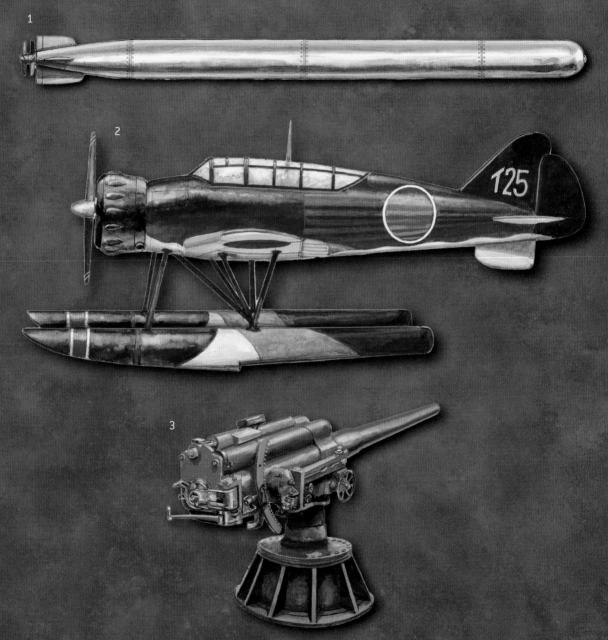

A major factor in the success of the IJN's submarine force was the development of a reliable and powerful torpedo. Capable of up to 51kn, the 21in Type 95 (**1**) was 23.5ft long and carried an 891lb warhead. The E14Y1 "Glen" (**2**) was the standard IJN submarine floatplane by 1942; performance was mediocre, with a top speed of 246mph and a very small bomb load, but the aircraft could be stowed in pieces in a small submarine hangar and then quickly assembled in as little as 6 minutes 23 seconds by an experienced crew. The E14Y1 was used to scout enemy bases, not ships at sea. The 5.5in/40 deck gun (**3**) used aboard most IJN submarines was the same weapon arming numerous other IJN ships including battleships and light cruisers; it was also the most common Japanese coastal-defense gun.

Japanese submarines were provided with a token short-range antiaircraft capability. The standard IJN short-range antiaircraft gun was the 25mm Type 96. This was deployed in single, dual, and triple-gun versions, with the dual mount being the most common aboard submarines. The 25mm Type 96 gun was a mediocre weapon which was difficult to train against fast-moving targets and aim, and suffered from a relatively slow rate of fire. Combined with the fact that submarines carried no dedicated fire-control system for engaging air targets, IJN submarines possessed a totally inadequate level of protection against air attack.

USN DESTROYER ASW WEAPONS

The standard ASW weapon used by the USN at the start of the Pacific War was the classic depth charge; a simple weapon, being nothing more than a can filled with explosives with a fuse that detonated using hydrostatic pressure at a preset depth. The USN began to develop its first depth charge in 1917; the final USN World War I depth charge could detonate at up to 300ft depth and had a 300lb charge. At the start of the Pacific War, however, USN depth charges had developed little with the exception of the Mark 7 with a 600lb TNT charge. Depth charges required a high degree of accuracy to kill a submarine – even the Mark 7 had to explode within some 10yd of a Japanese submarine to kill it and within some 30yd to damage it. Prior to a depth charge being deployed, the fuse had to be manually set according to orders from the bridge based on the estimated depth of the target. Often, in the confusion and tension of combat, the crew would neglect to set the depth, making the depth charge worthless.

USN early-war depth charges			
Weapon	Explosive weight	Sink rate	Settings
Mark 6	300lb TNT	8ft/sec; 12ft/sec from mid-1942	30–300ft; up to 600ft from mid-1942
Mark 7	600lb TNT	9ft/sec	50–300ft

Depth charges were usually deployed by racks positioned on the destroyer's stern. The racks were nothing more than inclined rails on which the charges rested, with mechanical devices to release them one charge at a time. A variant of the World War I-era Mark 1, the Mark 1 Mod 1 rack could hold five Mark 6 or three Mark 7 depth charges. These were standard on all USN prewar destroyers. The Mark 3 rack was introduced later in the war; it could hold eight smaller depth charges. Additional depth charges were stowed below deck and could be hauled up and loaded onto the rack by means of a block and tackle, which was an arduous process.

In order to expand a depth-charge pattern, destroyers carried depth-charge projectors, also known as K-guns. These were mounted on each beam and each fired a single depth charge. USN early-war destroyers usually carried 4–6 K-guns. The standard early-war projector was the Mark 6, introduced in 1941. By varying the weight of the black-powder charge in the expansion chamber, the depth charge could be fired at ranges of 60yd, 90yd, and 150yd.

USN DESTROYER ARMAMENT

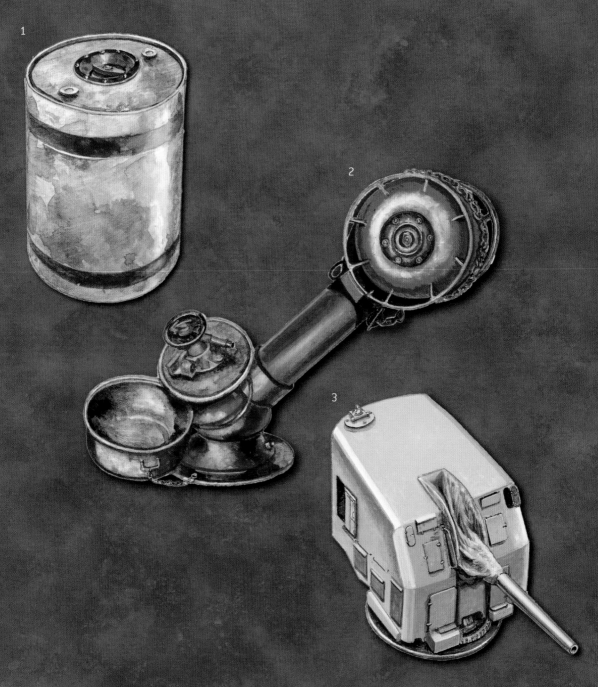

The most common USN antisubmarine weapon was the depth charge; a Mark 6 is shown here (1). This had a 300lb TNT charge and could be set to explode down to 300ft, equal to the operating depths of IJN submarines. The depth charge was deployed either by stern-mounted racks or by a projector such as the Mark 6 Depth Charge Projector shown here (2). This device could throw a depth charge up to 150yd from the destroyer. If a submarine was caught on the surface, US destroyers could use their 5in/38 guns (3). This dual-purpose weapon was highly accurate and had a high rate of fire.

Sonar was a destroyer's means of detecting a submerged submarine. There were two types of sonar carried by USN destroyers. Active sonar transmitted a sound wave through the water and an object in the water caused an echo to return. A skilled operator could use the time the echo took to return to calculate the distance to the underwater object, which was presumably a submarine. Sonar systems of this period were not very advanced and were subject to all manner of environmental factors that degraded their performance. Additionally, there was a "blind spot" to the potential submarine contact as the destroyer got nearer and then steamed over it. Passive sonar was simply a listening device employed to pick up sounds generated by a submarine, principally its screws. The sounds generated by the destroyer made use of passive sonar difficult, particularly above certain speeds. Therefore, active sonar was used to conduct depth-charge attacks.

From 1934, the standard USN prewar destroyer sonar was the QC, and this was carried by all modern destroyers going into the Pacific War. The QC operated at 24kHz with a power of up to 300W. Under perfect conditions on a destroyer steaming at 5kn, this translated to a theoretical maximum detection range of 3,635yd. Under realistic operational conditions, however, the detection range decreased sharply if the destroyer was moving above 10kn; and this was almost always the case for a destroyer escorting a task group. Even if detection was gained, the QC sent out a 14-degree-wide horizontal beam and an even wider vertical beam, which made gaining any depth information impossible.

A sailor sets the detonating depth on a 300lb Mark 6 depth charge mounted on a K-gun projector. (80-G-14940 courtesy of the Naval History & Heritage Command)

THE COMBATANTS

IJN SUBMARINE DOCTRINE AND TACTICS

Despite the important role assigned to submarines in the IJN's attrition strategy, the tactical components of this strategy were not seriously tested until a series of exercises in 1938 revealed severe shortcomings. IJN submarines had problems trying to get near heavily defended major fleet units or bases; during exercises, many were judged to have revealed their positions or were sunk. When they were forced to stay submerged to avoid antisubmarine forces, they were not able to receive radio messages that directed their movements. As a result of these experiences, IJN submarine tactics were altered. The importance of concealment was reinforced, but this resulted in submarine commanders becoming over-cautious, which explains how and why Japanese submarines could operate off busy harbors or bases yet report no contacts. The difficulty in maintaining surveillance of a well-defended base prompted the IJN to use submarine-launched aircraft in this role during the war.

IJN torpedo tactics highlighted the difficulty of launching effective attacks on fast, maneuvering groups of USN warships. The Japanese believed that the best position for a torpedo attack was from a distance of 1,650yd at an angle of 50–60 degrees off the target's bow, which required that the submarine maneuver to place itself in front of the target's course to achieve the optimal firing position. This was tactically very difficult, even when the target's course and speed were known; and because this was rarely the case, the standard IJN tactic was to form a scouting line across the projected path of an enemy task force in hopes of creating a favorable position for ambush. The feat of racing ahead of an enemy task force and gaining a favorable firing position was made all the more difficult by the standard Japanese tactic of firing torpedoes while submerged. Once submerged, a submarine was very slow and its ability to spot approaching ships was limited. This was demonstrated in a series of maneuvers in the Western Pacific during 1939–40 in which IJN submarines were unable to locate, track, and attack surface forces.

In February–March 1941, the 2nd Submarine Squadron conducted further exercises which confirmed the shortcomings in the IJN's prevailing submarine employment strategy. Among the problems was an insufficient number of submarines to conduct effective surveillance operations, inadequate submarine speed, and a great risk of detection by antisubmarine forces. The results of the exercises showed that enemy forces were able to leave port undetected by submarines, that submarines had difficulty tracking enemy forces once at sea, and that submarines had a very difficult time getting into firing positions. This was a prophetic description of IJN submarine operations for the first part of the war.

Further issues were highlighted when in March and July 1941, submarines of the 4th and 5th Submarine squadrons simulated attacks on well-guarded enemy fleet formations. The main lesson was the difficulty in attacking enemy units from close range because the submarine periscope was spotted, which simply confirmed the prevailing wisdom that submarines were vulnerable to alert antisubmarine defenses. The result was a very conservative attack doctrine in a navy known for its ethos of engaging the enemy at close quarters. Japanese submarine skippers invariably opted for maximum concealment at the expense of an aggressive attack. This translated to the tactical propensity to remain submerged and wait for a US ship to steam by and present itself as a target. Even if a contact was made, when operating against a well-screened enemy force, commanders usually opted for "submerged firing." In this scenario, the submarine would stay submerged, then expose the periscope for a final acquisition of target range and bearing, approach the firing point without using the periscope, and then fire on sound bearings.

In addition, the IJN never developed the tactic of concerted attack by its submarines; a tactic pioneered by the Germans, who called it the "wolf pack." The USN developed a similar tactic later in the war. In the case of the Germans, the wolf pack was directed by commands from a shore-based authority, much like the IJN concept of directing submarine operations. The USN took this a step further by using an embarked commander to direct repeated attacks on a single target. Both the Germans and Americans developed this tactic to attack and overwhelm slow-moving convoys. Despite the construction of several large submarines and later a light cruiser as dedicated submarine command platforms, the IJN never developed a similar capability to mass submarines quickly against a single target.

At the operational level, IJN submarines were directed to assume predesignated patrol areas or to patrol a picket line which was thought to be across the enemy's route of advance. In response to a changed situation, IJN submarines were directed by orders from ashore. This almost always resulted in submarines being ordered to and fro to different positions, most often based on faulty or dated intelligence. To patrol these new positions, a submarine had to conduct a surface transit during which it was at its most vulnerable. This risk had to be assumed, because without using its much higher surface speed a submarine would never get into a position to intercept an enemy task force.

This photo of the main control room gives an idea of the cramped conditions that existed aboard IJN submarines. Because crew comfort was not a design factor, IJN submarines were known for their arduous operating conditions. For example, unlike their USN counterparts, IJN submarines were not fitted with air-conditioning equipment, which made life in the tropics brutal. On a long patrol, such conditions were bound to affect the crew's morale and performance. (AirSeaLand Photos)

Coordination of the IJN's submarine operations was made possible by greatly improved communications equipment, which allowed shore commands to direct submarines at extended distances. High-frequency (HF) radio transmitters were the preferred method because these were able to transmit messages over great distances. In turn, the submarines could transmit detection reports at HF over great distances. However, the frequent use of HF transmissions was also a potential vulnerability because they could be detected by USN radio-interception units. The transmissions were eventually decoded, which gave the Americans high-quality intelligence on IJN submarine locations and intentions. In 1941 and for most of 1942, however, USN decryption efforts did not provide a flood of information on specific IJN submarine operations. Another byproduct of IJN submarine radio transmissions was the fact that by the late 1930s the USN could use radio direction-finding to geo-locate the transmitting submarine. During the early-war period, this was usually the best means the Americans had to enable them to gain an appreciation of IJN submarine locations.

At the strategic level, it is a myth that the IJN employed its submarines almost exclusively to support IJN fleet operations and ignored attacks on Allied commerce. Prewar exercises using Japanese merchant ships as targets had clearly demonstrated the potential vulnerability of commerce shipping. The IJN realized that attacks on enemy SLOCs were an integral part of modern naval warfare, but at the start of the war that was considered secondary to attacking the enemy's fleet. Japanese naval strategy was rooted in attacking the enemy's main fleet, and preparing for the climactic decisive battle, not attacking merchant ships. However, only a few months into the war, Japanese naval commanders realized that using submarines to attack the enemy's fleet was becoming increasingly difficult in the face of alert ASW defenses and so they gave attacking Allied merchant traffic a higher priority. This did not relieve the submarine force of the responsibility of supporting major IJN operations, however, and when combined with the relatively small numbers of IJN submarines in service, the result was that the mission of attacking enemy SLOCs was never pursued with much energy.

USN DESTROYER ASW DOCTRINE AND TACTICS

By the start of the Pacific War, USN ASW capabilities had advanced little since the end of World War I. In general, this was attributable to the financial straits the USN found itself in for most of the interwar period and the relatively low priority given to ASW. The USN had gained a wealth of ASW experience fighting German U-boats in 1917–18. The keys to defeating the U-boat threat were moving to a convoy system and then providing the convoys with an "umbrella" of protection from surface escort ships, and where range allowed, patrol aircraft flying dedicated ASW missions. The USN believed that these measures could be quickly implemented in a new conflict. The only major technological advance in ASW technology since World War I was the development of sonar, which promised to remove the cloak of invisibility from submarines. This was another reason for the USN's overconfidence regarding its ASW capabilities going into the war.

In the period before the war, USN Pacific Fleet destroyers did not devote much of their training time to ASW. Offensive torpedo drills against surface targets were rehearsed endlessly, but the accounts of USN destroyer commanders in the years before the Pacific War make clear that ASW was not a point of emphasis. The prewar experiences of Arleigh A. Burke, commonly acknowledged as one of the premier USN destroyer skippers during the Pacific War, are instructive. Burke was the executive officer of *Craven* during 1937–39, from the ship's commissioning to being moved to San Diego, and then commanding officer of *Mugford* in 1939–40, participating in the naval exercise Fleet Problem XXI in April 1940, and then being assigned to the Hawaiian Detachment in spring 1940 prior to the movement of the new Pacific Fleet to Pearl Harbor in 1941. Other than some ASW screening operations of the battle fleet in Fleet Problem XXI, there are no indications that either destroyer spent any meaningful time conducting ASW training.

The lack of a clearly identifiable ASW doctrine was also an issue. The USN came out of World War I with a solid ASW doctrine based on experience and embodied in the Statement of Antisubmarine Tactics from 1918. There appears to be no record of destroyer ASW doctrine from the interwar period, however; in fact, the 1939 Tactical Orders for Destroyers contains no mention of ASW at all and focuses solely on surface actions. Not until June 1943 did the Pacific Fleet issue a set of comprehensive fighting instructions covering all tactical considerations, and these were likely based on tactics, techniques, and procedures already in place. For ASW, the best method of screening major fleet units was based on the numbers of destroyers present, acoustic conditions, and awareness of the most favorable firing position for a Japanese submarine assuming the USN formation was steaming at 15kn and a Japanese torpedo run of 6,000yd at 36kn (this significantly underestimated the capabilities of the IJN's Type 95 torpedo). The distance between screening destroyers should not exceed 1.5 times the effective sonar range. All destroyers making a sonar or visual contact on a submarine were directed to proceed immediately to attack the contact. Known as a "distracting attack," its purpose was to disrupt the submarine's ability to

This photo shows the officers and much of the crew of the destroyer *Mugford* on the ship's forecastle, *c.*1939–40. Seated in the front row, center, is Lieutenant Commander Arleigh A. Burke, the ship's commanding officer. On a ship with good morale, the crew was close knit. Training was incessant; however, as was common for prewar USN destroyers, training for ASW operations was not a point of emphasis. (NH 55807 courtesy of the Naval History & Heritage Command)

launch an accurate attack and was to be carried out using guns, depth charges, or ramming to prevent the submarine from taking an aimed torpedo shot against a heavy ship. The destroyer was under orders to prosecute the attack until the submarine was definitely sunk or until the destroyer was ordered to rejoin the formation. Conditions permitting, the destroyer would launch a destructive attack with a full pattern of depth charges. Where possible, more than a single destroyer would be used to conduct a coordinated attack. This had the advantage of using one ship to make the attack and one or more other ships to maintain sonar contact. The senior destroyer officer present would determine whether the destroyers would use active or passive sonar.

While a USN task group was transiting, there were 12 zigzag plans in effect with prescribed course changes and the time and speed for each course change. In addition to screening destroyers, doctrine called for maximum usage of aircraft to conduct ASW patrols. Any aircraft sighting an enemy submarine was under orders to make an immediate attack unless there was a friendly destroyer within 1,500yd of the contact and no heavy ship within 10,000yd. This was deemed necessary to avoid disrupting the destroyer's ability to make a sonar-guided attack.

The favored early-war cruising disposition for a formation with a carrier (Disposition 5-LS) was used when the submarine threat was paramount, namely at night or in conditions of low visibility. This placed the carrier in the center of the formation, surrounded by an inner screen of five heavy ships (cruisers and battleships), all preceded by six destroyers deployed in a semicircle in advance of the formation. In high-visibility conditions, the destroyers were deployed in a tighter circle around the entire formation (Disposition 5-V). It was doctrine to steam in a zigzag during good visibility (including bright moonlight) in areas where a submarine threat existed.

COMBAT

THE HAWAIIAN OPERATION

Beyond the use of Type A midget submarines, it is little known that the IJN planned for its submarine force to play a major role in the Pearl Harbor attack. In addition to committing all of its fleet carriers, the IJN also allocated all of its modern fleet submarines to the operation. In fact, many IJN leaders thought the participation of the submarines was vital to the success of the operation because the carrier force was still untested and the operation itself carried with it a high risk of failure. The Pearl Harbor operation was a perfect opportunity for the IJN's submarine force to show its capabilities and exploit its doctrine of attacking USN fleet units. The submarines possessed the range to reach the Hawaiian Islands without difficulty, and the prewar doctrine of coordinating attacks on USN fleet units was ideal for striking USN ships as they fled Pearl Harbor following the carrier air raid. Much was expected of the submarine force, with many naval leaders expressing their belief that the submarines would prove more effective than the carriers. In fact, the submarine part of the Hawaiian Operation proved to be a total failure and a portent for future IJN submarine operations.

A total of 28 IJN submarines participated directly in the Hawaiian Operation. Three (*I-19*, *I-21*, and *I-23*) constituted the Patrol Unit and were assigned directly to the IJN carrier force. These submarines were deployed 50 miles ahead of the IJN carriers and had the dual mission of rescuing Japanese aviators unable to make it all the way back to their carriers and to protect the carriers from a potential American counterattack. Twenty IJN submarines were deployed in three groups around the island of Oahu (the location of Pearl Harbor) to interdict any potential USN

counterattack against the Japanese carriers and to mop-up remnants of the Pacific Fleet escaping from Pearl Harbor. The 1st Submarine Group (*I-9*, *I-15*, *I-17*, and *I-25*) was deployed to the north of Oahu; the 2nd Submarine Group (*I-1* to *I-7*) was deployed between Oahu and Molokai; the 3rd Submarine Group (*I-8* and *I-68* to *I-75*) was positioned south of Oahu. The three submarine groups departed their bases at Kure and Yokosuka starting on November 10. They did not head directly for the Hawaiian Islands, but made their way south to Kwajalein Atoll in the Marshall Islands to take on a full load of fuel and then headed to Hawaii.

In addition to the three groups positioned around Oahu, five submarines (*I-16*, *I-18*, *I-20*, *I-22*, and *I-24*) were assigned to the Special Attack Unit. Each submarine carried a Type A two-man midget submarine. These were ordered to enter Pearl Harbor hours before the air strike and then launch their torpedoes in the middle of the air raid when the defenders' degree of confusion would be at its greatest. Because the Special Attack Unit was not part of the plan to attack USN fleet units at sea, its activities will be briefly described here. The five midget submarines were launched in the early-morning hours of December 7 and proceeded slowly to the channel leading to Pearl Harbor. At 0342hrs, the worst fears of the Japanese aviators were realized when one of the midget submarines was spotted in the channel. Had the Americans reacted quickly, the element of surprise for the entire Pearl Harbor attack could have been jeopardized; but even after the same midget submarine was sunk by gunfire at 0645hrs, the Americans failed to go to full alert. One of the remaining four midget submarines did penetrate inside the harbor where it fired both its torpedoes, but both missed and it was rammed and depth-charged by the destroyer *Monaghan*. None of the other three midget submarines came this close to being successful. The efforts of the Special Attack Unit were entirely futile.

At least the Special Attack Unit saw action on December 7. Despite the fact that there were initially 25 Japanese submarines deployed around Oahu, where an abundance of American naval and merchant traffic was centered, there was a notable paucity of contacts reported by the lurking Japanese subs. This changed

The Farragut-class destroyer *Monaghan* pictured at Mare Island Navy Yard in February 1942. After sinking a Japanese midget submarine in Pearl Harbor on December 7, 1941, *Monaghan* was busy throughout 1942 on ASW screening duties. The ship was one of the destroyers that failed to protect the carrier *Yorktown* against submarine attack at the Battle of Midway. On June 20, 1943, *Monaghan* detected *I-7* off Kiska in the Aleutians and forced the submarine to run aground. (19-N-28346 courtesy of the Naval History & Heritage Command)

The Japanese used five Type A two-man midget submarines during the attack on Pearl Harbor but only one of these entered the harbor itself, where it fired both its torpedoes for no effect. This photograph (with the background obscured by the censor) shows that midget submarine after the attack, demonstrating the effects of depth charges and ramming. Despite this failure, the IJN continued to devote fleet submarines to ferry midget submarines to a whole series of targets where they achieved marginal results. (NH 54302 courtesy of the Naval History & Heritage Command)

early on December 10 when *I-6* spotted what was reported as a Lexington-class carrier in the Kauai Channel. From his flagship anchored at Kwajalein, Vice Admiral Shimizu Mitsumi ordered several submarines to chase down this lucrative target. In this first test of the IJN's ability to orchestrate submarine operations against a high-value target, the Japanese came off poorly. The target was actually the carrier *Enterprise*; yet despite utilizing their high surface speed, the submarines were unable to get a good firing solution over a period of two days. Two submarines reported getting off long-range submerged torpedo shots, but both were unsuccessful. In exchange, *Enterprise* accounted for the first IJN submarine loss of the war when the carrier's Dauntless dive-bombers spotted and attacked *I-70* on the morning of December 10 some 200 miles northeast of Oahu. The attack caused enough damage to prevent the submarine from diving, allowing other Dauntlesses to sink *I-70* later in the day.

While the Japanese submarines were unable to account for a single USN warship, they did have some very limited success against merchant targets. In the days following the Pearl Harbor attack, *I-9*, *I-10*, and *I-26* each sank a merchant ship off the Hawaiian Islands. The three submarines of the Patrol Unit, and the four submarines of the 1st Submarine Group were ordered to join *I-10*, which had been conducting reconnaissance of American islands in the South Pacific, and *I-26*, which was performing the same mission off the Aleutians, and head to the US West Coast to attack merchant shipping.

The 3rd Submarine Group departed the Hawaiian Islands on December 17, followed by the 2nd Submarine Group on January 11. Before departing, *I-4* sank a merchant ship on December 14, and on December 17, *I-7* used its E14Y1 floatplane to conduct a daring dawn scouting mission over Pearl Harbor to confirm the results of the air raid. The results of the Hawaiian Operation, during which the IJN deployed a total of 28 fleet submarines and five midget submarines, were extremely disappointing from the Japanese perspective. No USN ships had been damaged or sunk, and only a handful of merchant ships were sunk. In return, the IJN had lost a fleet submarine and all five of its midget submarines.

OPERATIONS IN EARLY 1942

Japanese expansion continued in early 1942 on all fronts, and IJN submarines supported all these operations. The range of IJN operating areas expanded until they included a huge chunk of the world's oceans from the eastern coast of Africa to the West Coast of the United States. This immense expanse, combined with the relatively small numbers of submarines available, prevented the Japanese from concentrating submarines at a decisive area.

In the early months of 1942, older Japanese submarines were active in the Dutch East Indies and began to deploy into the Indian Ocean to attack Allied merchant traffic. Because Allied defenses were less intense in the Indian Ocean, Japanese attacks there on Allied shipping were generally more effective than in other theaters. Despite the need to send submarines into refit and the choice to send a small number into the Indian Ocean, the IJN was able to keep a number of submarines on station off the Hawaiian Islands. Three of the submarines that had delivered midget submarines on December 7 (*I-18*, *I-22*, and *I-24*) were ordered to return to the Hawaiian Islands after refueling and receiving supplies at Kwajalein. They departed on January 3 and joined the seven submarines of the 2nd Submarine Group still operating in the area.

THE ATTACK ON *SARATOGA*

On the morning of January 9, *I-18* sighted a Lexington-class carrier and a heavy cruiser near Johnston Island headed west. Rear Admiral Yamazaki Shigeteru on *I-7* ordered the nearby submarines of the 2nd Submarine Group to establish a north–south picket line and head to the west. This effort paid dividends when at 1740hrs on January 11, *I-6*, operating in the northern part of the picket line, sighted a Lexington-class carrier, one cruiser, and two destroyers some 420 miles southwest of Oahu. After maneuvering to get into a favorable firing position, *I-6* launched a spread of three Type 89 torpedoes from 4,700yd from an angle of 80 degrees. One of the torpedoes hit the carrier *Saratoga* amidships on the port side, which flooded three boiler rooms. The Japanese skipper reported the carrier as sunk, based on two loud explosions heard on the submarine's hydrophones followed by what was interpreted as the sounds of the ship breaking up. In reality, *Saratoga* took on 1,100 tons of water, but was never in danger of sinking. The carrier was able to steam back to Pearl Harbor and then proceeded to the US West Coast for repairs. However, the first major IJN submarine success of the war was critical because it forced *Saratoga* to miss the carrier battles of Coral Sea and Midway in early May and early June, respectively.

The IJN doctrine of coordinating submarine attacks on USN fleet units had finally demonstrated promise by placing several submarines in the same water space as a high-value target. It must be pointed out, however, that *I-6* benefited from a large degree of luck when *Saratoga* literally steamed across the path of the submerged submarine. *Saratoga*'s screening destroyers failed to locate *I-6* before or after the attack.

Another Japanese submarine success was recorded on January 23 when *I-72* sank the USN fleet oiler *Neches* 135 miles west of Oahu. This was a significant loss given the small numbers of fleet oilers available at the time; a shortage reflected by the fact that the loss of *Neches* forced the cancellation of a planned carrier raid on Wake Island.

OPERATIONS IN DIVERSE AREAS

A hallmark of IJN submarine operations during 1942 was the propensity to assign submarines distant operating areas – a clear violation of the IJN's precept that the primary focus of submarine operations should be direct support of fleet operations. These distant operations were not efficient because they required long transit times and once the submarines arrived, the prospects for success were limited.

The nine submarines sent eastward to take up positions off the US West Coast operated in assigned patrols areas covering the coastline from Washington State south to San Diego. The results of this deployment were again disappointing. No USN ships were attacked, much less sunk and the Japanese only claimed five merchant ships as sunk. Most of the nine submarines returned to Kwajalein during January 11–15. Despite this lack of success, the IJN persisted in sending two other groups of submarines to the US West Coast into October 1942, but the successes of the submarines devoted to these deployments continued to be limited to a few merchant ships. The height of futility was reached in September when the floatplane from *I-25* conducted two totally unsuccessful incendiary attacks on forests in Oregon.

Another example of the IJN's propensity to use its submarines in boutique operations was the series of midget-submarine attacks. The Japanese were not discouraged by the failure of the five midget submarines at Pearl Harbor, and in fact considered it a success because they believed one of the five had torpedoed a battleship inside the harbor. They intended to repeat the operation in the Indian Ocean. Five submarines (*I-10*, *I-16*, *I-18*, *I-20*, and *I-30*) departed for the Indian Ocean in late April 1942, three carrying midget submarines and the other two carrying floatplanes. After *I-10*'s floatplane conducted a series of reconnaissance flights at locations in East Africa, on May 31 the Japanese launched a midget-submarine attack on the Diego Suarez naval base at the northern tip of Madagascar, where British naval units had been located. The two midget submarines that were launched damaged the battleship *Ramillies* and sank the tanker *British Loyalty*. (Of note is the fact that *I-30* went on to conduct the first round-trip to Europe to collect technology and personnel from the Germans.) Another five submarines (*I-21*, *I-22*, *I-24*, *I-27*, and *I-29*) were dispatched to conduct a midget-submarine attack on the east coast of Australia. The attack on Sydney on May 31 was a total failure – the three midget submarines launched sank only the Australian accommodation ship *Kuttabul*. The ten submarines committed to conduct these midget-submarine attacks contributed nothing to the IJN's principal strategic goal of defeating the USN. Had they been focused on the upcoming Midway operation, and been deployed correctly, they would have had the potential to make a significant impact.

More confusion about the priority of IJN submarine operations followed after a change of command of the Sixth Fleet on March 16, 1942 when Admiral Shimizu was relieved by Vice Admiral Komatsu Teruhisa. The new commander agreed with the views of many IJN submarine officers that the prewar strategy of using submarines to attack USN fleet units and to scout American naval ports was no longer viable in the face of an alert enemy. The new priority was attacking merchant shipping.

DEBACLE AT MIDWAY

After a brief raid into the Indian Ocean in April 1942, the IJN turned its attention to dealing with the USN. Tense negotiations between the Naval General Staff and the staff of the Combined Fleet resulted in a decision to undertake sequential offensive operations in the South Pacific and then in the Central Pacific. The main operation was to be the Central Pacific drive, designed by Yamamoto to be a decisive clash in which the IJN would crush the remnants of the USN in the area of Midway Atoll. IJN submarines were slated to play a major role in this battle.

The prelude to the Midway operation was an operation to seize Port Moresby on the southeastern coast of New Guinea in early May. Eight Japanese submarines were used to support this operation. Two of the eight were coastal submarines deployed near Port Moresby, while the other six were fleet boats: *I-22*, *I-24*, *I-28*, and *I-29* were positioned some 250 miles southwest of Guadalcanal to protect the flank of the invasion force; *I-21* and *I-27* were also dispatched, but were assigned post-invasion reconnaissance missions against Australian and other ports in the South Pacific. These eight submarines contributed nothing to Japanese efforts.

The Port Moresby operation went well at first, with the island of Tulagi being occupied on May 3; but the Japanese were unaware of the presence of two USN carrier groups in the area and these engaged the Japanese covering force on May 7 and the main IJN carrier force the following day. The result was a tactical stalemate in which the IJN lost the light carrier *Shōhō* and suffered heavy damage to the fleet carrier *Shōkaku* in exchange for sinking the carrier *Lexington* and damaging the carrier *Yorktown*. The only involvement by IJN submarines was on May 2 when *I-21* was attacked by USN carrier aircraft within some 32 miles of *Yorktown*. The submarine was not damaged, but neither did it sight the carrier group. At no point during the battle did an IJN submarine spot an American warship. On its return to the major fleet base at Truk in the Carolines, *I-28* was torpedoed and sunk by the USN submarine *Tautog* on May 16.

The entire Japanese conduct of the planning and execution of the Midway battle was sloppy in the extreme. An example was the participation of the submarine force. If this was designed to be a decisive battle, then the contribution of the submarine force should have reflected that. However, both from a force allocation and deployment perspective, it did not. A total of 14 submarines were assigned to support the operation, but of these only 11 were deployed on two picket lines between Midway and Pearl Harbor to give warning of the approach of USN forces. The submarines selected to patrol the two picket lines were older boats that had material and readiness issues. Even before the battle, a submarine expert on the Naval General Staff predicted that the submarines assigned this key mission would not be up to the job. Six other submarines were dispatched to support the secondary operation in the Aleutians.

The most critical submarine deployment was that of the 3rd and 5th Submarine squadrons which were assigned to the two picket lines and charged to detect and attack any USN units attempting to intervene in the Japanese occupation of the atoll. Picket Line "A" was some 700 miles southeast of Midway and stretched for 200 miles; Picket Line "B" was about 700 miles east of Midway and stretched 200 miles along a northeast–southwest axis. It was planned that the 11 submarines patrolling these picket lines would arrive on May 30 – five days before the scheduled first air attack on Midway. However, several boats from the 3rd Submarine Squadron were not able to depart Kwajalein on schedule because of equipment malfunctions, and thus arrived late to their assigned stations. Three of the boats (*I-171*, *I-174*, and *I-175*) were assigned to support the planned flying-boat reconnaissance of Pearl Harbor. Two other boats (*I-121* and *I-123*) were assigned to refuel the flying boats at French Frigate Shoal, but when USN units were discovered at the refueling area, the operation was canceled on May 31. This prevented any pre-battle aerial reconnaissance of Pearl Harbor and meant that several of the boats were late assuming their picket positions. Another submarine assigned to take part in the operation, *I-64* from the 5th Submarine Squadron, was sunk by the American submarine *Triton* en route Kwajalein on May 16.

The net result of poor planning and poor readiness was that the picket lines were not implemented on schedule and the three USN carriers that were deployed to ambush the Japanese invasion force moved through the area undetected. For the IJN, ridden with "Victory Disease" from its unbroken string of successes since the start of the war, the late deployment of the picket lines did not appear to be a problem because the Midway plan assumed that the IJN would gain strategic surprise, and that the USN would not react until after Midway was attacked. This was obviously not the case. On June 4, the carriers *Enterprise*, *Yorktown*, and *Hornet* ambushed the IJN's carrier force and crippled all four fleet carriers (*Akagi*, *Kaga*, *Sōryū*, and *Hiryū*). All four later sank, making the battle a clear American victory. In the course of the carrier battle, the Japanese carriers did manage to launch two air strikes. Both hit *Yorktown*, the second placing two torpedoes in the carrier and leaving the ship crippled and dead in the water only 150 miles from Midway.

In response to the disastrous events of June 4, Yamamoto ordered his submarines to shift positions in an effort to attack the USN carriers. Orders were issued for the submarines in Picket Lines A and B to move to a new picket line designated "C" by the morning of June 5. The new position, 500 miles east of Midway, was still nowhere near the position of the USN carriers. The next day, orders were issued for the submarines to move to a new picket line less than 100 miles west of Midway. The submarines were not able to reach the new position until June 10 or 11, but before then Yamamoto issued new orders moving the submarines back to the east of Midway in response to information that the USN carriers were there. This constant movement based on faulty intelligence resulted in nothing of substance. Only *I-169* even sighted USN forces late on June 7 and was unable to launch an attack.

THE EXPLOITS OF *I-168*

One IJN submarine accounted for the only major Japanese success in the battle. *I-168*, under Lieutenant Commander Tanabe Yahachi, was assigned to patrol in the vicinity of Midway. Tanabe was able to issue some useful pre-battle reports and on June 4, conducted a brief six-round bombardment of the atoll. Tanabe was thrust into the spotlight of history when he received orders to attack the crippled *Yorktown*. On June 5, a Japanese aircraft spotted the listing carrier some 150 miles north-northeast of Midway. Because Tanabe's was the nearest submarine to the location, he was given the mission of finishing the carrier off. He made for the contact during daylight on June 5 using his best submerged speed. After dark, he surfaced and began a visual search. At 0530hrs on June 6, a lookout spotted the carrier, 11 miles away and screened by six USN destroyers: *Hammann* was alongside providing power for the salvage crews on board *Yorktown* and the other five circled about 1 mile out using their active sonars. Tanabe began a slow approach and by about noon was within 600yd of the carrier. Tanabe feared this was too close for his torpedoes to arm, so he ordered that *I-168* silently circle around until the boat was in an optimal firing position 1,200yd away. Finally, at 1330hrs, Tanabe fired a four-torpedo salvo at the carrier set in a tight spread for maximum destructive effect. Two of the torpedoes passed under *Hammann* to strike *Yorktown*; a third hit the destroyer, which broke apart and sank in 4 minutes with the loss of 81 crew. The fourth torpedo missed. This final damage was too much for *Yorktown* and the carrier sank the next morning.

OVERLEAF
One of the salient IJN successes of the war was *I-168*'s attack on the carrier *Yorktown* northeast of Midway on June 6, 1942. After a skillful approach during which none of the six USN screening destroyers detected the submarine, *I-168* fired four torpedoes at *Yorktown* with the destroyer *Hammann* alongside. Hit by a single torpedo, *Hammann* broke apart and sank in four minutes; two torpedoes hit the carrier, which sank the following day.

The destroyer *Hammann* pictured at Charleston Navy Yard, South Carolina, in January 1942, just before the ship transferred to the Pacific. The destroyer is painted in Measure 12 (modified) camouflage. Upon arriving in the Pacific, *Hammann* fought at the Battle of Coral Sea before being sunk at the Battle of Midway – one of only two USN destroyers sunk by Japanese submarine attack in 1942. (NH 96828 courtesy of the Naval History & Heritage Command)

The Type KD6A/KD6B boats, such as *I-68*, shown here, were very active during the first year of the war. Three were sunk in 1942, and all were lost by 1944. *I-68*, the most successful boat of the type, was sunk by a USN submarine in July 1943. (© IWM MH 5950)

Yorktown about to make the ship's final plunge. This view looks forward, with *Yorktown*'s forefoot in the center and the large torpedo hole evident. *Yorktown*'s starboard forward 5in gun gallery is in the left center, with two 5in/38 gun barrels sticking out over its edge. When the wreck of the carrier was examined in May 1998, both guns were still in position. (NH 106000 courtesy of the Naval History & Heritage Command)

After failing to detect *I-168*, the five surviving USN destroyers launched a fierce counterattack. Some 60 depth charges and seven hours later, *I-168* was in bad shape with low supplies of battery power and air remaining, and a leak that threatened to force the boat beyond its safe diving limit. Tanabe surfaced at dusk to recharge *I-168*'s batteries. The destroyers soon spotted the submarine and brought it under fire, but the boat submerged and successfully escaped. Tanabe was heralded as a national hero upon his return to Japan, and he certainly gave an excellent performance. His activities also highlighted the weakness of USN ASW capabilities at this point in the Pacific War and the difficulty of protecting even a stationary target against a well-handled submarine.

ORDEAL AT GUADALCANAL

While the IJN pondered what to do after the Midway disaster, the USN seized the initiative. On August 7, the Americans landed on Tulagi and Guadalcanal islands in the southern Solomons. This was intended as the first step of an operation to isolate and seize the major Japanese South Pacific bastion of Rabaul, located on the island of New Britain. Tulagi was captured after a brief, sharp fight, but the fate of the operation to take Guadalcanal was in the balance for months. The struggle for Guadalcanal was the most prolonged campaign of the Pacific War and drew in the bulk of the IJN and USN. This included the Japanese submarine force, which made a significant impact on the course of events for the only time in the Pacific War.

The IJN was caught off-guard by the Guadalcanal landing, and took a while to mount a major counteroffensive. Only a couple of coastal submarines were in the area when news of the landing reached Rabaul, but soon seven boats from the 1st Submarine Squadron (*I-9*, *I-15*, *I-17*, *I-19*, *I-26*, *I-31*, and *I-33*) were ordered to the South Pacific and three boats from the 3rd Submarine Squadron (*I-11*, *I-174*, and *I-175*) were shifted from operating areas off Australia to the Solomons. These ten submarines joined the five submarines of the 7th Submarine Squadron already operating out of Rabaul. Later, the old cruiser submarines of the 2nd Submarine Squadron were deployed to the Solomons. The only modern submarines not moved to the Solomons were the ten boats of the 8th Submarine Squadron, based at Penang and tasked with attacking shipping in the Indian Ocean. The Sixth Fleet commander, Vice Admiral Komatsu, moved his flagship to Truk to direct the operation.

Despite the commitment of most of the IJN's fleet boats to support operations at Guadalcanal, the initial Japanese attempts to prevent the Americans from reinforcing the island were entirely fruitless. By late August, the Combined Fleet had gathered enough strength in the South Pacific to mount a major operation designed to cripple USN forces off Guadalcanal. This resulted in the Battle of the Eastern Solomons, fought on August 24. In support, Komatsu deployed seven fleet submarines in a picket line northeast of Guadalcanal to intercept USN carriers entering the battle area. Another picket line with three submarines was deployed some 150 miles south of Guadalcanal, near Rennell Island. The three minelaying submarines (*I-121*, *I-122*, and *I-123*) were deployed east of Malaita Island, and a coastal submarine (*RO-34*) was deployed in Indispensable Strait between Guadalcanal and Malaita. The intent was to cut off US reinforcements to the island and to report on and attack approaching USN carriers.

The USN force was centered on the three carriers of Task Force 61 – *Wasp*, *Saratoga*, and *Enterprise* – which the main IJN submarine picket line northeast of Guadalcanal failed to spot before the battle. On the evening of the battle, the seven IJN submarines patrolling this picket line were ordered to shift 100 miles to the south, and the three submarines south of Guadalcanal were ordered to move to the east and link with the new position of the larger picket line. During the battle, *I-17* found herself in the middle of Task Force 61's operating area. The boat was attacked twice during the morning of August 23 by Dauntless dive-bombers, but suffered only minor damage. The following day, *I-17* was again caught on the surface by dive-bombers,

I-26, shown here in 1943, was the IJN's third-highest-scoring submarine in terms of tonnage sunk, accounting for nine merchant ships and the light cruiser *Juneau*. The boat was also responsible for damaging the carrier *Saratoga* on August 31, 1942. *I-26* survived until October 26, 1944, when the submarine was lost to probable operational causes during the Battle of Leyte Gulf. (© IWM MH 5952)

but suffered no damage. Early on August 25, *I-15* and *I-17* spotted a carrier, but were unable to close for an attack. Komatsu ordered the boats to maintain contact, and other nearby boats to join the attack. Later that same day, Komatsu ordered both groups to return to their original patrol positions. The next day, *I-17* again spotted a carrier, but on this occasion was detected by escorting USN destroyers. *I-17* went deep, and suffered no damage under depth-charge attack.

The frustrations of the IJN submarine force were on full display at the Battle of the Eastern Solomons. The problem with maneuvering slow submarines to attack fast-moving fleet units was evident. If the IJN submarines were to have any hope of carrying out their orders to move to a new patrol area in a timely manner, they had to do so on the surface, thus exposing them to potential attack. Of course, any orders to change location were only as effective as the intelligence upon which they were based. Most Japanese intelligence on USN fleet movements was derived from aerial reconnaissance, but this usually arrived late or proved inaccurate. The result was a stream of orders moving submarines from picket line to picket line with no tangible result. However, as the campaign for Guadalcanal dragged on, the Japanese were able to discern USN operating patterns and movements, which gave them enough insight to place their submarines in USN operating areas. Eventually, this was bound to result in attacks on USN fleet units.

The danger inherent in operating in the same area as IJN submarines became apparent on August 31. Because of his orders to operate south of Guadalcanal unless in contact with the enemy, the commander of the USN carrier force, Vice Admiral

Frank Jack Fletcher, was stuck in a box 150 miles long and 60 miles wide east and southeast of San Cristobal Island. This was in the same area as some of Komatsu's submarines. On August 27, American carrier aircraft detected a Japanese submarine only 50 miles from the carriers. They attacked the submarine but without success. On August 31, radar on the carrier *Saratoga* and the escorting battleship *North Carolina* detected a contact, which was investigated by the destroyer *Farragut*. Nothing was found. Nevertheless, Fletcher maneuvered his task group so that a little over four hours later it returned to within 30 miles of the earlier suspicious radar contact. The destroyer *MacDonough* gained a sonar contact on a submarine close by; this was followed by a periscope sighting only 30ft off the destroyer's bow. *MacDonough* moved to drop two depth charges (which in their haste the crew did not arm) on the contact. The destroyer was so close that the ship's hull was heard to scrape against the hull of the submarine. The boat was *I-26* but the contact by the escorting destroyer was too late – a salvo of six torpedoes, fired from 3,800yd, was already on its way to *Saratoga*.

The 888ft-long *Saratoga* was infamous for being unable to turn quickly. The carrier tried to turn to starboard, but was unable to avoid the danger. One torpedo hit the carrier abreast the island on the starboard side. Just like in January, the big ship easily absorbed the impact of a single torpedo and was in no danger of sinking. However, the damage to the carrier's propulsion system required three months' repair work in the yards. This put *Saratoga* out of action during the climactic period of the Guadalcanal campaign, including the Battle of the Santa Cruz Islands on October 25–27 in which the two USN carriers available (*Enterprise* and *Hornet*) were forced to fight four opposing Japanese carriers.

In spite of having clearly revealed its position, *I-26* survived the attentions of the destroyers *MacDonough* and *Phelps*, both of which reported sonar contacts and dropped depth charges. In order to cover the retreat of *Saratoga*, the destroyer *Monssen* remained in the area of the contact to keep the submarine submerged until after dark. *Monssen*'s claim to have sunk the submarine was incorrect, and *I-26* survived to inflict more pain on the Americans.

The destroyer *Phelps* at Pearl Harbor, late May 1942, following the Battle of Coral Sea and shortly before the Battle of Midway. A Porter-class destroyer, *Phelps* was optimized for surface warfare, carrying a main battery of eight 5in/38 guns. At the start of the war, the destroyer carried only two stern-mounted depth-charge racks for ASW work. (80-G-66124 courtesy of the Naval History & Heritage Command)

Saratoga photographed under repair at Tongatapu, Tonga, in September 1942 after being torpedoed by *I-26* on August 31. The carrier's list is deliberate, to bring the damaged starboard side out of water. (80-G-12967 courtesy of the Naval History & Heritage Command)

THE DEATH OF *WASP*

As painful as the loss of *Saratoga* was to the USN, worse was to come in September 1942. USN carriers were still under orders to remain southeast of Guadalcanal, but the carrier admirals chafed under these restrictions. Rear Admiral George Murray, commanding Task Force 17 built around the carrier *Hornet* and battleship *North Carolina*, decided to ignore these restrictions in order to provide better support to the US Marines on Guadalcanal. On September 6, Task Force 17 was located south of Guadalcanal and northwest of Espiritu Santo. This was in the area of the IJN's submarine picket line, and specifically in the sector of *I-11*. The IJN boat was patrolling submerged when it detected Task Force 17 on its hydrophones. Commander Shichiji Tsuneo made an undetected approach; none of the escorting six destroyers picked up the threat. At 1249hrs, he made another periscope check and found *Hornet* dead ahead at a range of only 765yd. He fired all four bow tubes, and then ordered a dive to 200ft and the boat rigged for silent running. Within 3 minutes, two explosions were heard. Shichiji claimed hits on an Enterprise-class carrier.

The real story was much different. Despite the short range, the attack by *I-11* was unsuccessful. A patrolling USN Avenger torpedo bomber spotted what the pilot believed was a submarine's conning tower inside the task force's destroyer screen and dropped a depth charge on the threat, which was actually the incoming torpedoes, causing two to detonate. *Hornet* made a hard turn to port to avoid a third torpedo. Two hours later, the destroyer *Russell* located *I-11* on sonar and dropped six depth charges. These were placed accurately, and the resulting damage was extensive. The boat suffered a leak in its stern and lost 80 percent of battery power, going to 490ft before the crew could restore control. After repairs, the boat surfaced seven hours later. Unable to continue his patrol, Shichiji ordered a return to Truk on the surface. The boat survived two attacks by Catalina flying boats over the next two days, but reached Truk safely.

On September 10, Komatsu ordered *I-9*, *I-15*, *I-17*, *I-19*, *I-21*, *I-24*, *I-26*, and *I-33* to patrol between Ndeni (Nendo) and San Cristobal islands. This ensured that what the Americans now called "Torpedo Junction" would be well monitored when the next large USN force came through. The carriers *Wasp* and *Hornet* were both assigned to escort a large reinforcement convoy headed for Guadalcanal. Not only did the Americans have to contend with the possibility of submarine attack, but the IJN's carrier force was known to be active to the north. On the morning of September 13, a Japanese H8K "Emily" long-range flying boat reported a USN task force 345 miles south-southeast of Tulagi. *I-9* and another submarine were already in this area, but a further six boats were ordered to join them and form a picket line.

On September 15, the American carriers were active in the vicinity of *I-15* and *I-19* in the middle of the IJN submarine picket line. *I-19*, under the command of Lieutenant Commander Kinashi Takakazu, detected a large USN force by hydrophone at 1250hrs. Kinashi came to periscope depth to make a quick visual check, but saw nothing. At 1350hrs, he raised his periscope again and this time sighted a carrier, a heavy cruiser, and several destroyers 9 miles away. The carrier and its escorts were headed northwest and zigzagging at 16kn. At 1420hrs, Kinashi got the break he was looking for when the carrier changed course to conduct flight operations. This placed the Americans on a course directly toward him. At 1445hrs, Kinashi took his shot with a full salvo of six Type 95 torpedoes from a range of 985yd. None of the carrier's six escorting destroyers detected either of the two submarines.

At this range, there was insufficient time for *Wasp* to take evasive measures when three torpedo wakes were spotted off the starboard bow. The first torpedo hit near the bow, followed by a second just forward of the island. These cracked the aviation-fuel storage tanks and flooded the forward magazines. Within 20 seconds, there was a third explosion, but it remains unclear if this was from a third torpedo or from the detonation of aviation-fuel vapors. It soon became clear that the damage to *Wasp* was fatal. The carrier took a starboard list and went down by the bow. The cracked aviation-fuel storage tanks spilled gasoline into the water, which produced a blanket of fire around the stricken vessel. The shock of the explosions caused the fueled and armed aircraft in the hangar bay to erupt in flames. Minutes after the torpedo hits, three massive fuel-vapor-induced explosions from deep within reduced the forward part of the carrier to ruins. At 1520hrs, the crew was ordered to abandon ship. Almost six hours later, the carrier sank after being scuttled by destroyer torpedoes. The loss of *Wasp*, along with 193 crew, was nothing less than a disaster and left a single USN carrier (*Hornet*) operational in the Pacific.

OVERLEAF

I-19's deadly salvo of six torpedoes on September 15, 1942 not only sank the carrier *Wasp*; three of the torpedoes continued on to the *Hornet* task group located several miles away. One of the torpedoes hit the destroyer *O'Brien*, as shown here, which eventually resulted in the ship's loss. Another torpedo hit the battleship *North Carolina*, shown in the background, and put one of the USN's most modern battleships out of action for two months.

As bad as this was for the Americans, things soon got worse. *Hornet* and the carrier's escorts were steaming 5 miles away. The three torpedoes fired from *I-19* that missed *Wasp* proceeded toward the *Hornet* task force. At 1452hrs, one hit *North Carolina* on the port side underneath the forward 16in turret. The 891lb warhead on the Type 95 torpedo caused massive damage – a 32ft-long by 18ft-high hole 20ft below the waterline – that resulted in a small list, but *North Carolina* was able to maintain 25kn and keep the battleship's place in formation. The massive ship was in no danger of sinking, but was out of action for the next two months, which included the carrier clash at Santa Cruz and the two vicious mid-November surface battles (the First and Second Naval Battles of Guadalcanal). The carnage continued at 1454hrs when another of the three torpedoes hit the destroyer *O'Brien*. The damaged destroyer made it to the base at Espiritu Santo the following day, and then proceeded to Nouméa, New Caledonia, for temporary repairs. However, the ship's structural integrity had been fatally compromised, and on October 19, while returning to the United States for permanent repairs, *O'Brien* broke in two and sank off Samoa.

The success achieved by *I-19* on September 15 was noteworthy, but the continued hope of the Combined Fleet's staff that IJN submarines could stop or reduce the flow of US reinforcements to Guadalcanal went unfulfilled. On September 29, *I-4* damaged the cargo ship *Alhena*, the only time Japanese torpedoes hit a supply ship bound for Guadalcanal. The continued futility of Japanese submarine operations against American supply lines in the South Pacific, most of which were in the form of defended convoys, is noteworthy and undermines the notion that the Japanese had only to devote submarines to attacking American SLOCs to be successful.

I-176 vs *CHESTER*

The next Japanese submarine success was scored by *I-176* on October 20. Task Force 64, with the battleship *Washington*, heavy cruisers *Chester* and *San Francisco*, light cruisers *Helena* and *Atlanta*, and eight destroyers, was steaming in Torpedo Junction. The task force split in the early evening and *I-176* spotted a column of cruisers and four destroyers at 2040hrs. Despite the fact the group was zigzagging at

19kn, *I-176* soon got into firing position. At 2115hrs, the submarine launched a full salvo of six torpedoes at what the skipper identified as a Texas-class battleship. In fact, this was *Chester* at the rear of the column. One of the torpedoes hit the cruiser on the starboard side in an engine room at 2120hrs. The hit caused a loss of power, and *Chester* came to a stop. Within 90 minutes, power was restored and the cruiser was able to depart the area at 8kn. The escorting destroyers conducted a three-hour attack on *I-176*, but the submarine was eventually able to surface and escape. *Chester* was out of action for over a year, missing the First and Second Naval Battles of Guadalcanal in mid-November when the services of a heavy cruiser would have been extremely beneficial for the Americans. The captain of *I-176* was Lieutenant Commander Tanabe – the same man responsible for sinking *Yorktown* while commanding *I-168*.

In an unsuccessful attempt to increase the pressure on USN supply lines, Rear Admiral Yamazaki, commander of the 1st Submarine Squadron, was given unified

The heavy cruiser *Chester* pictured off Mare Island Navy Yard on August 6, 1942 following overhaul. Before *Chester* could be committed to the intense series of surface actions around Guadalcanal, the cruiser was torpedoed by *I-176* on October 20 and missed the rest of the campaign. (19-N-32461 courtesy of the Naval History & Heritage Command)

I-176 pictured running trials on July 31, 1942. The new submarine was given to Lieutenant Commander Tanabe, hero of the *Yorktown* attack at Midway. He was responsible for damaging the heavy cruiser *Chester*, but left the boat before it sank the USN submarine *Corvina* (the only USN submarine sunk by a Japanese submarine during the war) on November 16, 1943 and before being sunk by USN destroyers in May 1944. (AirSeaLand Photos)

command of all Japanese submarines around Guadalcanal in September. In October, the Japanese carried out another ground attack to capture the airfield on Guadalcanal. This action was accompanied by a major fleet operation to crush the USN, which resulted in the Battle of the Santa Cruz Islands on October 25–27, during which the IJN gained a significant victory. Ten submarines were deployed in support of the operation in two groups, but they contributed nothing other than the attack on *Chester* on October 20. The problem again was the constant shifting of picket lines in response to dated or poor intelligence. Three submarines (*I-15*, *I-21*, and *I-24*) did sight American ships and got off torpedoes, but none hit their target. On October 27, *I-21* fired three torpedoes at what the captain identified as a "Colorado-class" battleship 150 miles south of Indispensable Reef. The actual target was *Washington* and the battleship was undamaged when a single torpedo exploded in its wake. *I-21* escaped damage from the escorting destroyers by going deep. *I-21* had more success on November 9 when it slammed a single torpedo into a Liberty ship off Nouméa. The ship was towed into Nouméa, but was deemed a total loss.

JUNEAU'S DEMISE

In November, the IJN prepared its largest and final attempt to crush the USN at Guadalcanal. In support, Rear Admiral Mito Hisashi (the new commander of the 1st Submarine Squadron as of October 22) deployed ten submarines around the island. Three of the boats (*I-16*, *I-20*, and *I-24*) continued the Japanese infatuation with midget submarines. Three more (*I-15*, *I-17*, and *I-26*) were positioned southwest of San Cristobal Island to attack American reinforcement convoys, and the final four (*I-122*, *I-172*, *I-175*, and *RO-34*) were deployed northeast of San Cristobal Island for the same purpose. A midget submarine from *I-20* damaged a cargo ship off Guadalcanal on November 7.

I-26 scored the last major success for the IJN's submarine force during the campaign on November 13. The First Naval Battle of Guadalcanal, fought during the early-morning hours of November 13, resulted in heavy losses to an American task force ordered to stop a Japanese bombardment of the airfield on the island. The morning following the battle, the remnants of the USN force gathered to transit southeasterly down Indispensable Strait and head for the New Hebrides. The force consisted of the light cruiser *Helena*, deployed at the head of the column, and then the heavy cruiser *San Francisco*. Abeam of the heavy cruiser was the light cruiser *Juneau*. Two destroyers were deployed 2 miles in front of the cruisers as an ASW screen. At 0950hrs, *Sterett*

The light cruiser *Juneau* photographed off New York City on June 1, 1942 before departing to the South Pacific. After being damaged in the First Naval Battle of Guadalcanal on November 13, *Juneau* was torpedoed and sunk later the same day by the veteran *I-26* with horrendous loss of life. The wreck of the cruiser was discovered in April 2018. (19-N-31264 courtesy of the Naval History & Heritage Command)

reported a sonar contact and delivered a depth-charge attack. This attack was against a phantom contact. An hour later, *I-26* was lining-up a firing solution on *San Francisco*, which was steaming at 18kn and zigzagging. The three torpedoes fired at *San Francisco* missed, but one continued to *Juneau*, and hit the light cruiser in the bridge area on the port side. *Juneau* had been damaged by a torpedo hours before in the same area, and the result of the second hit was catastrophic. Following a magazine explosion, the light cruiser disintegrated and sank. The loss of life was horrific. Of the crew of 700 men, all but ten lost their lives either in the explosion or during the lackluster rescue operations, which did not commence for several days.

THE END OF THE CAMPAIGN

The whole nature of the Japanese submarine campaign in the South Pacific changed on November 16, when Komatsu ordered his boats to assume responsibility for supplying the stranded Japanese garrison on Guadalcanal. The situation for the Japanese troops on Guadalcanal was especially tenuous because US command of the air and intensifying surface operations around the island made supply by destroyers, the preferred method, too perilous. The garrison was virtually starving, and Yamamoto felt duty-bound to do whatever he could to get supplies through. The only method with a chance of success was using submarines. Accordingly, on November 16 all available I-boats were ordered to Rabaul. Under the command of Rear Admiral Mito, they began supply missions immediately.

The first supply run to Guadalcanal was conducted by Tanabe on *I-176*. At first, 13 submarines were assigned to these missions, and 28 submarine supply runs had been completed by February 1943 (when the Japanese evacuated Guadalcanal). These were enough to keep the garrison going. The submarines with aircraft hangars had the most capacity – some 50 tons. This was sufficient for two days of supply for the garrison. In total, some 1,115 tons of supplies were delivered and 2,000 troops evacuated by submarine.

There were costs. The first was to the morale and efficiency of the submarine crews that were pulled off offensive operations to carry out the hated "mule" operations. *I-3* was lost to PT-boat attack on December 9; *I-4* was lost to a US submarine on December 21; and *I-1* was lost on January 29, 1943 after being attacked by two New Zealand corvettes. With the Japanese evacuation of Guadalcanal in February 1943, the campaign came to an end. The IJN had suffered a devastating defeat, but the question remains – were the operations of the submarine force through 1942 successful, or did they reflect the ineffective efforts of a force unable to meet its mission?

The saga of the transport ship *Alchiba* displayed the futility of the IJN's midget-submarine operations. For the efforts of three fleet submarines and the loss of eight midget submarines, the Japanese succeeded in damaging only two cargo ships off Guadalcanal. This is *Alchiba* on fire off Lunga Point, Guadalcanal, after being torpedoed on November 28 by a midget submarine from *I-16*. *Alchiba*'s crew ran the ship aground, which saved the vessel. *Alchiba* was torpedoed again on December 7, this time by a midget submarine from *I-24*. The ship was salvaged and served for the duration of the war. (USMC 66457 courtesy of the Naval History & Heritage Command)

STATISTICS AND ANALYSIS

The conventional wisdom is that the IJN's submarine force was ineffective during the war because it failed to sink a significant number of USN warships. Another generally held belief is that the Japanese would have been better off had they sent their submarines to attack Allied SLOCs instead of focusing on USN fleet units. The former is not entirely true, as the examination below will show, and the latter is patently untrue.

The effectiveness of IJN submarines against USN major fleet units has been misjudged. In spite of its well-known successes, epitomized by the sinking of *Yorktown* and *Wasp*, the IJN submarine force has received insufficient credit. Because the carrier was the USN's most important fleet unit in 1941–42, and because Japanese submarines were focused on attacking them, the record of success by Japanese submarines against USN carriers needs to be examined.

Of the six USN carriers in the Pacific from December 7, 1941 through December 1942, three were sunk or damaged by Japanese submarines. As shown by the table below, this amounted to a period of some 31 percent from December 7, 1941 until the end of 1942 when these ships were not available because of submarine attack. The damage to *Saratoga* from two different submarine attacks meant the carrier was out of the war for most of 1942. Of the four carrier battles during that time, *Saratoga* missed all but one. *Yorktown* was on the verge of being salvaged after being heavily damaged by two aerial torpedoes at Midway when the carrier was sunk by *I-168*. Though it is hard to imagine *Yorktown* returning to service in 1942 after being so heavily damaged, the carrier's sinking at the hands of *I-168* guaranteed it missed the rest of 1942. *Wasp*

was the last USN carrier to reach the Pacific in 1942, but had a short-lived combat career. After missing the carrier battle of the Eastern Solomons in August, *Wasp* was sunk the following month. This placed the USN on the edge of disaster when only a single carrier (*Hornet*) was operational in the entire Pacific.

Japanese submarine successes against USN carriers 1941–42

Carrier	Months in service	Months lost to submarine attack
Lexington	6	0 (sunk by IJN air attack, May 8, 1942)
Saratoga	4	9
Yorktown	6	6 (sunk by *I-168*, June 7, 1942)
Enterprise	13	0
Wasp	4	3.5 (sunk by *I-19*, September 15, 1942)
Hornet	7	0 (sunk following IJN air attack, October 27, 1942)
Totals	*40*	*18.5*

The torpedo damage from *I-6*'s January 11 attack kept *Saratoga* from participating in the pivotal battle of Midway in early June. In this view, *Saratoga* arrives at Pearl Harbor from the US West Coast on June 6, 1942. The carrier departed the following day to join the carriers *Enterprise* and *Hornet* near Midway, bringing them replacement aircraft to strengthen their heavily attrited air groups. (80-G-10121 courtesy of the Naval History & Heritage Command)

Much of the IJN submarine force's success against USN fleet units was due to favorable circumstances or USN operational shortcomings. *Yorktown* was dead in the

This is the carrier *Wasp* burning and listing after being torpedoed by *I-19* on September 15, 1942 while operating in what was known to American sailors as "Torpedo Junction." The loss of *Wasp* was a potential catastrophe because it left *Hornet* as the only operational USN carrier in the entire Pacific. The IJN failed to exploit this advantage, however. (80-G-16331 courtesy of the Naval History & Heritage Command)

water when the Japanese received intelligence about the carrier's location, allowing *I-168* to find its target and make a skillful attack. Most of the other successful attacks were due to the USN continuing to expose its key units to submarine attack by steaming back and forth in "Torpedo Junction" between August and November 1942. This unfortunate operating pattern explains the successful attacks on *Wasp*, *North Carolina*, *O'Brien*, and *Chester*. Not until late November did the Americans stop needlessly transiting Torpedo Junction unless it was to go to a specific destination or for a combat mission.

In comparison to their successes against USN carriers, the record of IJN submarines against other USN fleet units looks sparse. However, in September 1942, they did torpedo one of the three modern USN battleships in the Pacific (*North Carolina*), forcing it to miss the decisive surface battles off Guadalcanal in mid-November. Additionally, IJN submarines put a heavy cruiser (*Chester*) out of action in October, also forcing it to miss the November battles, and sank a light cruiser (*Juneau*) as it retreated from that same November battle.

The question still needs to be asked: why wasn't the IJN submarine force more successful? It is almost inconceivable that Japanese submarines could patrol for weeks off Hawaii, the US West Coast, or near Guadalcanal and report no attacks or even contacts. The primary reason was the conservative tactics adopted by Japanese submarine captains as a result of prewar exercises that supposedly revealed submarines to be vulnerable. IJN submarines stayed submerged during daylight hours when in their patrol area and even preferred to fire torpedoes while submerged, using sound bearings. Because they were submerged, they literally relied on USN ships to steam close enough to the submarine to become targets. It is to the credit of the submarine crews that they tried so hard to make their unworkable prewar tactics work, and that they occasionally scored important successes. It is to the discredit of their commanders that they did not understand the basic capabilities of the submarines under their command and ardently clung to outmoded tactics. The USN's prewar submarine force also began the war with passive tactics, including submerged torpedo firings, but when these tactics were shown to be ineffective, they were discarded.

THE MYTH OF THE LOST OPPORTUNITY AGAINST ALLIED SLOCS

The IJN was criticized after the war for failing to attack Allied SLOCs. Given that they were so long and thus difficult to defend, the Japanese could have reaped a rich harvest, or so the thinking goes. In fact, the IJN submarine force never had the capabilities to execute an anti-shipping strategy. In March 1942, Komatsu did just that – he changed the priority of Japanese submarine targeting from attacking naval units to attacking shipping; but, as had already been shown early in the war off the US West Coast, Japanese submarines were not numerous or aggressive enough to inflict significant losses on Allied shipping. The conservative IJN submarine tactics were equally ineffective against naval units and shipping, and in the vast distances of the Pacific Ocean targets were relatively scarce to start with.

When Komatsu shifted to attack merchant shipping, he sent ten fleet boats to augment the few forces already operating in the Indian Ocean. These boats were more effective than those operating in the southern and eastern Pacific, but such a small number could never bring significant results. Off Guadalcanal, Japanese submarines were continually tasked with attacking American SLOCs to the island; but in using their passive tactics against better-defended targets (usually convoys, not merchant ships steaming independently), they proved almost totally ineffective against American supply lines. As the war progressed, there was absolutely no reason to suggest that attacking Allied SLOCs would have been anything more than a nuisance given the shrinking number of IJN submarines available and the growing efficiency of USN ASW forces. Additionally, Komatsu never had the option of devoting all his forces to anti-shipping attacks, because any major IJN fleet operation still demanded the participation of submarines.

In a broad perspective, it can be said that the IJN submarine force was as effective as it could have been in 1942 given the relatively small numbers of submarines available and the Japanese reluctance to jettison ineffective tactics. What the Japanese could be criticized for was continuing to use fleet submarines for missions that promised little in return, such as being used to ferry midget submarines. The most egregious example of misusing submarines was employing them to supply bypassed garrisons, but this was a requirement levied on IJN submarine commanders from above.

THE AMERICAN RESPONSE

As uneven as the performance of the Japanese submarine force may have been, it has completely concealed the USN's inability to screen its heavy units from submarine attack early in the war. In 1941, the IJN lost three submarines; only one of these losses was the result of USN ASW forces, and this was *I-70*, sunk by carrier aircraft, not by USN destroyers.

A better idea of the ineffectiveness of USN ASW forces can be gathered from the results of 1942. During this year, the IJN lost 17 submarines. Not one of these was the result of a successful attack by a USN destroyer on a submarine attacking a task force. On top of that, not once was a Japanese submarine sunk after it launched an attack on a USN task force. The best defense against Japanese submarines was the high speed at which most task forces transited, but this defense was minimized when USN task forces continually operated in the same submarine-infested waters.

IJN submarine losses 1941–42		
Submarine	**Date**	**Circumstances**
I-70	December 10, 1941	Sunk by USN carrier air attack northeast of Oahu
RO-66	December 17, 1941	Sunk by collision off Wake Island
RO-60	December 29, 1941	Ran aground off Kwajalein
I-60	January 17, 1942	Sunk by British destroyer in Sunda Strait
I-124	January 20, 1942	Sunk by Australian surface ships near Darwin
I-73	January 27, 1942	Sunk by USN submarine near Midway
I-23	Late February 1942	Lost to unknown causes off Oahu
I-28	May 17, 1942	Sunk by USN submarine off Truk
I-64	May 17, 1942	Sunk by USN submarine south of Shikoku Island
I-123	August 29, 1942	Sunk by USN minelayer near Guadalcanal
RO-33	August 29, 1942	Sunk by Australian destroyer off Port Moresby
RO-61	August 31, 1942	Sunk by USN destroyer *Reid* in the Aleutians
I-33	September 26, 1942	Sunk by accident at Truk
I-22	October 6, 1942	Sunk by USN aircraft near Guadalcanal
I-30	October 13, 1942	Sunk by mine off Singapore
RO-65	November 3, 1942	Sunk by US aircraft at Kiska
I-15	November 10, 1942	Sunk by USN minesweeper off Guadalcanal
I-172	November 10, 1942	Sunk by USN destroyer minesweeper *Southard* in Eastern Solomons
I-3	December 9, 1942	Sunk by PT boat off Guadalcanal
I-4	December 21, 1942	Sunk by USN submarine south of Rabaul

AFTERMATH

The IJN submarine force had its most successful year of the war in 1942. However, the trends established in 1942 translated into the decline of the IJN's submarines for the remainder of the war. In 1943, IJN submarines remained focused on attacks on Allied merchant traffic. However, increasingly fleet submarines were tasked to act as resupply ships, leaving fewer boats available for other missions. Resupply missions were expanded after the evacuation of Guadalcanal to a number of points on New Guinea, followed by a growing list of other garrisons as the Americans used an island-hopping strategy to bypass Japanese garrisons.

The IJN continued to build several types of submarines during the war, but never settled on a single design to facilitate true mass-production. This is the Type B3 boat *I-58*, which was not completed until September 1944. The device on the aircraft hangar in front of the sail is a Type 22 radar, which IJN submarines finally began receiving in 1944. *I-58* scored the last IJN submarine success of the war when the boat sank the heavy cruiser *Indianapolis* on July 30, 1945. (© IWM MH 5951)

For the remainder of the war, losses increased at the hands of the growing numbers of American ASW forces. The efforts to supply and then evacuate the small Japanese garrisons on Attu and Kiska in the Aleutians mirrored the final stages of the Guadalcanal campaign. Eventually, 15 IJN submarines were committed to this effort, and four were lost. In November 1943, nine submarines were sent to counter the American invasion of the Gilbert Islands in the Central Pacific. The growing efficiency of American ASW forces was clearly displayed by sinking six of these. In return, the only Japanese submarine success was the sinking of an escort carrier (*Liscome Bay*) by *I-175* on November 24. The only bright spot in 1943 was a push of eight boats into the Indian Ocean late in the year, which accounted for a large number of Allied

merchant ships. During that year, 29 Japanese submarines were lost, but 37 new ones joined the fleet. In return, a paltry 56 Allied merchant ships were sunk.

The year 1944 saw the IJN fight and lose two "decisive" battles. In February, the major fleet base at Truk, home to the Sixth Fleet for most of the war, was abandoned in the face of US air power. IJN submarines operated from Japan for the remainder of the war. Not until May did the first Japanese submarine receive radar. By that time, American ASW forces were employing new equipment and tactics that made the survival of any Japanese submarine on patrol uncertain. This was demonstrated by the fate of the 13 submarines deployed in the Central Pacific in May. Guided by cryptologic intelligence, a single USN destroyer escort sank six in the span of 12 days. When US forces invaded the Marianas in June, 28 submarines operated in support of the operation. Using superior intelligence, radar, and aggressive tactics, these provided invaluable reconnaissance of the IJN's Combined Fleet as it approached the battle area, and then sank two of the three Japanese fleet carriers committed to the operation. The IJN did deploy 20 submarines to the battle, but they contributed nothing and ten were lost.

When the Americans invaded the Philippines in October, the IJN committed virtually all its remaining ships. Only 14 submarines remained to join the fight. These sank a destroyer escort and damaged a light cruiser and an escort carrier, but this was little compensation for the IJN's massive defeat at the Battle of Leyte Gulf, which marked the effective end of the IJN's surface fleet.

The desperate straits in which the IJN found itself by late 1944 led to the final phase of the IJN's submarine campaign. This featured using the remaining submarines to carry *kaitens*, which were manned versions of the Type 93 torpedo. Because the torpedoes now had a very sophisticated guidance system in the form of a human suicide pilot, the IJN thought this was a weapon of tremendous promise. I-boats could carry up to six *kaitens*. In practice, the *kaiten* proved to be ineffective, accounting for only a USN fleet oiler and a destroyer escort. Total IJN submarine losses in 1944 came to 58 boats.

USN ASW capabilities grew exponentially during the war through a powerful combination of better intelligence, more ASW assets including escort carriers, destroyer escorts, and ASW aircraft, and better weapons including the Mark 24 mine (actually the first homing torpedo) and the hedgehog mortar (a thrown-ahead ASW weapon). In April 1945, IJN *kaiten* operations were reduced in the face of heavy losses. For example, off Okinawa in April, eight of 11 submarines were lost for no result. The last major success, the sinking of the heavy cruiser *Indianapolis* on July 30, 1945, was scored by *I-58* in the Philippine Sea. By the end of the war, only a handful of Japanese submarines remained. The IJN's submarine force was never able to replicate its successes in 1942, when it was a factor to be reckoned with.

In response to increased USN ASW capabilities, the IJN developed submarines with extremely high submerged speeds. *I-202*, pictured here, was a Type ST unit. Their 19kn submerged speed was achieved through the adoption of a streamlined hull combined with new, more powerful electric motors and high-capacity batteries. Three units were completed before the end of the war, but none conducted an operational patrol before Japan's surrender. (AirSeaLand Photos)

BIBLIOGRAPHY

Boyd, Carl & Yoshida Akihiko (1995). *The Japanese Submarine Force and World War II*. Annapolis, MD: Naval Institute Press.

Carpenter, Dorr & Norman Polmar (1986). *Submarines of the Imperial Japanese Navy*. Annapolis, MD: Naval Institute Press.

Commander-in-Chief US Pacific Fleet (June 1943). *Current Tactical Orders and Doctrine*.

Evans, David C. & Mark R. Peattie (1997). *Kaigun: Strategy, Tactics, and Technology in the Imperial Japanese Navy 1887–1941*. Annapolis, MD: Naval Institute Press.

Hashimoto Mochitsura (2010). *Sunk: The Story of the Japanese Submarine Fleet 1941–1945*. Joshua Tree, CA: Progressive Press.

Januszewski, Tadeusz (2002). *Japanese Submarine Aircraft*. Sandomierz: Mushroom Model Publications.

Kizu, Tohru, ed. (2014). *History of Japanese Submarines*. Tokyo: Ships of the World.

Lacroix, Eric & Linton Wells (1997). *Japanese Cruisers of the Pacific War*. Annapolis, MD: Naval Institute Press.

Military History Section, Headquarters, Army Forces Far East (1952a). *Submarine Operations December 1941–April 1942. Japanese Monograph 102*. Office of the Chief of Military History, Department of the Army.

Military History Section, Headquarters, Army Forces Far East (1952b). *Submarine Operations in the Second Phase Operations Part I, April 1942–August 1942. Japanese Monograph 110*. Office of the Chief of Military History, Department of the Army.

Military History Section, Headquarters, Army Forces Far East (1952c). *Submarine Operations in the Second Phase Operations Part II, August 1942–March 1943. Japanese Monograph 111*. Office of the Chief of Military History, Department of the Army.

Morison, Samuel Eliot (1975). *The Struggle for Guadalcanal August 1942–February 1943. History of United States Naval Operations in World War II, Volume V*. Boston, MA: Little, Brown & Co.

Orita, Zenji & Joseph Harrington (1976). *I-Boat Captain*. Canoga Park, CA: Major Books.

Prange, Gordon W. (1981). *At Dawn We Slept*. New York, NY: McGraw-Hill Book Co.

Sternhall, Charles M. & Alan M. Thorndike (1946). *Antisubmarine Warfare in World War II*. Washington, DC: Operations Evaluation Group, Office of the Chief of Naval Operations, Navy Department.

Whitley, M.J. (1998). *Destroyers of World War Two*. Annapolis, MD: Naval Institute Press.

www.combinedfleet.com

Surrendered IJN destroyers and submarines pictured at Kure after the end of World War II. Of the IJN's submarine force, only five older fleet boats and four more modern ones survived the war. Among those in this view are *I-36*, *I-47*, *I-53*, and *I-58*. (NH 94884 courtesy of the Naval History & Heritage Command)

INDEX